Ali Edwards

A DESIGNER'S eye

for scrapbooking with patterned paper

CREATING
Keepsakes
SCRAPBOOK MAGAZINE

A child's world is fresh and new and beautiful, full of wonder and excitement. It is our misfortune that for most of us that clear-eyed vision, that true instinct for what is beautiful and awe-inspiring, is dimmed and even lost before we reach adulthood. If I had influence with the good fairy, who is supposed to preside over the christening of all children, I should ask that her gift to each child in the world be a sense of wonder so indestructible that it would last throughout life, as unfailing antidote against the boredom and disenchantments of later years, the sterile preoccupation with things that are artificial, the alienation from the sources of our strength.

Rachel Carson

contents

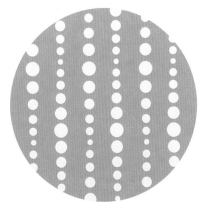

foreword
CLEARLY, ALI'S THE EXPERT

IF YOU'VE NEVER MET ALI, PREPARE YOURSELF because you're about to get to know her. You see, in everything she does—scrapbooking, teaching, designing, and even writing this book—she shares herself.

I mean it—I've never met a soul who can so completely (and genuinely) give of herself.

Don't believe me? Check out her pages and you'll find that her gift for giving comes through her scrapbook pages. She willingly shares her life—her real life, seemingly insignificant moments—on each page. I love that about Ali.

And one of the most important gifts Ali brings is her ability to teach complex ideas in easy, concise, bite-sized lessons. All of a sudden, after reading this book, the mystery of combining different patterns is clear and understandable—thanks, Ali.

It's nice to know that I don't have to be a graphic designer, because Miss Ali is right here, lending me her eye, her help and her genuine enthusiasm.

So sit back and prepare yourself to meet someone who I'm lucky enough to call friend. I've no doubt that by the time you've finished with this book, she'll be your friend, too.

Enjoy,

contributors

Miley Johnson

Miley Johnson was inducted into the *Creating Keepsakes* Hall of Fame in 2004. Says Miley, "I love the artistic side of scrapbooking. But above the art, above all the cool tools and embellishments, is the story of each page. These stories are what inspire and motivate me to scrapbook." Miley lives in Omaha, Nebraska, with her husband and four children.

Jamie Waters

Jamie Waters was inducted into the *Creating Keepsakes* Hall of Fame in 2003. Says Jamie, "I love scrapbooking as a way to record funny memories, little quirks or serious feelings and thoughts about my family." Jamie lives in South Pasadena, California, with her husband and four children.

Annie Weis

Annie Weis was inducted into the *Creating Keepsakes* Hall of Fame in 2005. "Scrapbooking has changed the way I see, feel, think and write," Annie says. "While I was in the academic world, I didn't even realize how important visual arts, photography and hands-on creativity were to me. Now I can't seem to live without them." Annie lives in Oakland, California, with her husband and two daughters.

Vanessa Reyes

Vanessa Reyes was inducted into the *Creating Keepsakes* Hall of Fame in 2003. Says Vanessa, "I love the look of joy on my children's faces as they flip through a scrapbook. I love creating art, and I love the feeling of excitement when I see cool new patterned papers! I think that scrapbooking is a way for me to give my family the very important gift of special memories and family stories." Vanessa lives in Lake Point, California, with her husband and two children.

bring back
THE FUN

I am a self-proclaimed ARTSY-GRAPHIC scrapbooker.

what in the world does that mean? Basically, on monday, I can be CLEAN, GRAPHIC and PRECISE; on Tuesday, I'll be all about painting, collage and experimental techniques. And on Wednesday, it may be a wonderfully interesting combination of both. This is what fills me up. This awesome opportunity for variety. For flexibility. For play. It's one of those things that makes me oh so happy.

Another thing that seems to be making me happy these days are patterned papers. So many beautiful options. So many fresh, inspiring way to tell my stories. When I create with patterns, I give myself permission to place squares next to circles next to stripes next to florals, to use a little or a lot — to simply play.

As I travel the country, scrapbookers continually tell me that creating layouts with patterned papers is a challenge. They express a bit of fear about combining patterns, unsure how or why to choose patterns for their projects.

Whether you love to cover your layouts with bunches of patterns or enjoy choosing one simple strip as an accent, this book will encourage you to embrace the idea that patterns are cool, fun and super-inspiring (and so _not_ scary). I hope you'll feel empowered to play, to tell your story, and to embrace the glorious imperfection inherent in my favorite form of Art.

AL;

capture life. create art. ™

goofy

SIMON

YOUR MALL

You Are Here

FOR you

love is the vital essence that pervades and permeates, from the center to the circumference, the graduating circles of all thought and action. love is the talisman of human weal and woe — the open sesame to every soul.

elizabeth cady stanton

circles

PATTERNED PAPER

*Circles. Simple, lovely shapes. Round and soft, without any
sharp points or hard edges.*

I've been thinking a lot about circles these days. And about life. About
cycles and seasons and the nature of things. Scrapbooking seems to do
that to me. Makes me think, reflect, remember, and then brings me
back to the present. I see the world differently since I became a scrapbooker. I see more patterns, more cycles, more little moments, how
everything seems linked together in one way or another.

A circle can be very mathematical and precise, as in *"A circle is the
locus of all points equidistant from a central point"* (Math2.org).
Or it can be much more organic and emotional, as in *"Living things
all have a moment at which they become 'alive.' That beginning of
life marks the first point on the circle of life"* (The Franklin
Institute). I think that's why I love using circles in design—one little
circle can communicate so many different things.

YOUR MALL BY ALI EDWARDS

SUPPLIES ON OPPOSITE PAGE *Textured cardstock:* Bazzill Basics Paper; *Patterned papers:* Magic Scraps (blue circles), Scenic Route Paper Co.
(green circles); *Letter stickers and circle accents:* Scrapworks; *Rub-on stitches:* Autumn Leaves; *Stamping ink:* Stampin' Up!; *Rubber stamp:*
Stampers Anonymous; *Pen:* American Crafts.

In scrapbooking, circles are *everywhere*. Embellishments both thick and thin. Patterned paper. Punches. Paper cutters. Tags. You can even purchase paper that's already cut into the shape of a circle. I tend to reach for circle embellishments for almost every page I create. I love the contrast of hard-edged papers with soft circles placed here and there.

Circle-patterned paper can feature polka dots; open, enveloping circles that tend to look more like lines; compact circles where each one touches the next; large and small circles mixed in together and on and on. So much awesome variety in every size and color. *Are you ready to play?*

Circles often represent the following ideas in art. Revise this list, add to it, make it your own.

- TOGETHERNESS
- COMPLETION
- ENERGY
- UNITY

- FAMILIARITY
- JOURNEY
- CHILDHOOD
- INFINITY
- ROUND

- ENTHUSIASM
- CYCLES
- FOREVER
- FUN

Choose circle prints because you love them and because of the stories they can help you tell on your pages. In this chapter, I'll show you how.

Most of them were bought 10-15 years ago - some in Portland, most in Berkeley - and they have since traveled the world. During the last four years (and the last three garages), they've been sitting in storage. Last year, I went through all my boxes and sold about five hundred of my least favorite books, so now I'm down to the core of the collection. Three shelves and four hundred years of wonderful American literature: Brockden Brown, Cooper, Hawthorne, Melville,

twain, James, Cather, Faulkner, Hurston and many, many more. One big shelf with stacks of books on linguistics, literary criticism, gardening, design, business, travel and history. I like these little stacks of non-fiction: the titles beckon to be read and I'm always tempted to pull a book out and sink into the couch. I spent my birthday putting all of them up on my brand new shelves, and what a good day that was.

I've missed you, my books. I'm so glad I have you back in my life again.

MY BOOKS BY ANNIE WEIS

why this works: Two large blocks of patterns and "white" space (black in this case) set a strong **foundation** upon which Annie added her journaling and photos. Ribbon corners and the hard edge of type on the top right and the "b" in "books" in the bottom-left corner keep your eye within the page.

SUPPLIES *Textured cardstock:* Bazzill Basics Paper; *Patterned papers:* Scenic Route Paper Co. and Scrapworks; *Letter stickers:* Heidi Grace Designs, me & my BIG ideas and Memories Complete; *Border stickers and ribbon:* Scrapworks; *Metal spiral clip:* 7gypsies; *Rub-ons:* Heidi Swapp for Advantus and KI Memories; *Computer font:* Manita, downloaded from the Internet; *Other:* Brads.

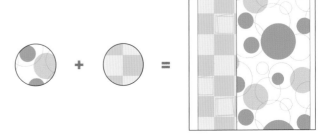

summer 2005

"Mom—come here!" I thought I'd walk in and see crazy bubble beard or something. But instead— kissy bubbles. aaahhww— how sweet is that?!!

kissy bubbles

KISSY BUBBLES BY JAMIE WATERS

why this works: This layout features a pleasing proportion of patterns: one large, one medium and one thin strip. A nice muted color combination lets the photos take center stage. Also, the large circle accents work well as a home for the title and repeat the circles from the dominant pattern.

SUPPLIES *Patterned papers:* Chatterbox, American Crafts and Autumn Leaves; *Cork tag:* Creative Imaginations; *Letter stickers:* American Crafts (white), Li'l Davis Designs ("b," "e," "s" and "l"), Autumn Leaves ("u"), Doodlebug Design ("b" on tag), Anna Griffin ("b"); *Paper tags:* Autumn Leaves.

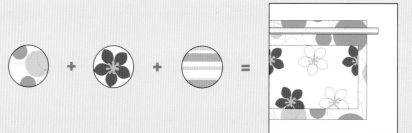

groovy

masterpiece

totally

easter
EGGS

awesome

TRADITION (tre·dish·ən) 1. passing down
of beliefs and customs from one generation
to the next 2. long-accepted and reoccurring
practices associated with specific occasions

@the beach
2o05

good times.

Easter at the beach - how cool is that? Dad and I had a little getaway weekend in
Portland and you had the awesome opportunity to celebrate Easter with grandma
and grandpa. And you got to do one of my favorite things: dye the eggs. Grandma,
being the creative genius that she is, got you all set up with cool white bowls filled
with color (and then she took photos of course). Grandpa helped you dye the eggs -
enjoying your interest in the colors & in the eggs themselves. You dipped. You named
the colors. You investigated. You dropped the eggs into the bowls. Some of the eggs
cracked (but you know what - no one cared because that is part of the process & the
fun - I love that grandma and grandpa get that). You took your responsibility as the
official "egg-colorer" very seriously. Dude, you are so cool.

EASTER EGGS AT THE BEACH BY ALI EDWARDS

why this works: Repeating a variety of circle patterns creates unity. Punched patterns and
photos create a gathering that complements the larger photos on the bottom and top right.

SUPPLIES *Patterned papers:* Making Memories; K&Company; foof-a-La, Autumn Leaves; Gin-X, Imagination Project; Scrapworks; *Rub-on:* Scrapworks; *Stickers:*
7gypsies and Making Memories; *Computer font:* Myriad Condensed, downloaded from the Internet; *Pen:* American Crafts.

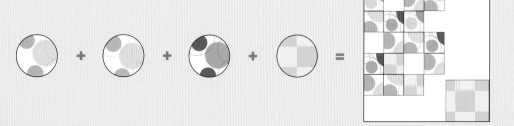

IT'S A BIG WORLD, BABY BY VANESSA REYES

why this works: Vanessa artfully combined a variety of elements by giving them homes within circles and squares. Remember to pull colors from your patterned papers that complement the overall color scheme. And don't be afraid to go over the edges of those circle accents.

SUPPLIES *Patterned papers:* Chatterbox and Pebbles Inc.; *Rub-ons:* Making Memories and Scrapworks; *Metal-rimmed tag, chipboard letter, page pebbles and woven corner:* Making Memories; *Heart token:* Doodlebug Design; *Epoxy letter:* K&Company; *Metal letter:* American Crafts; *Ribbon:* Making Memories and May Arts; *Other:* Jewelry tag and handmade paper.

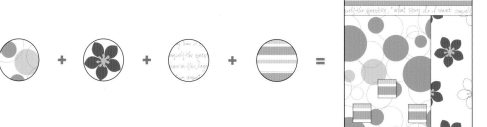

Yum—so proud of you for entering this Kidspace. Was sponsoring a Mini Iron Chef Challenge. Lots of goodies available to make the most delicious choco bite milk. You had a bath and devoured it.

YUM BY JAMIE WATERS

why this works: Jamie pulled a color from the photo—the red in the straw—and selected patterned papers that repeat that color (and notice how it's not exactly the same color). As a finishing touch, she added accents that repeat colors in the second patterned paper. Little bits of color can have a big visual impact.

SUPPLIES *Patterned papers, die cuts and rub-ons:* KI Memories; *Letter stickers:* American Crafts; *Phrase sticker:* K&Company; *Pen:* American Crafts.

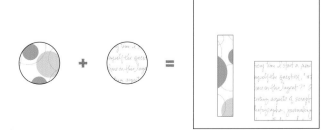

BOOGIE JOY BY ALI EDWARDS

why this works: Sometimes all a page needs is just a bit of pattern. Here, a gathering of photos is complemented by two small blocks of circle patterns and one additional piece of a circle-patterned paper for one of the "o's" in "Boogie." The three patterned areas make a nice visual triangle, tying all the areas of the layout together.

SUPPLIES *Textured cardstock:* Bazzill Basics Paper; *Patterned papers:* Danny O (large circles), K&Company; KI Memories (small circles); *Letter stickers:* Making Memories; *Rub-on:* foof-a-La, Autumn Leaves; *Pen:* American Crafts; *"Joy" accent:* K&Company.

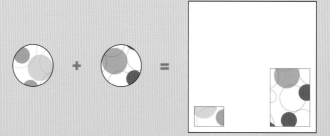

BARE FOOTED BOYZ BY MILEY JOHNSON

why this works: Circle accents are great additions to layouts with circle patterns. Miley's page repeats several circle elements, including circle brads, circle punches (my favorite is the one near the bottom-right corner, where there's a circle in a photo corner), and cork circles. Also, notice how Miley choose a very "loose" circle pattern—it creates a nice contrast to all the other stripe patterns on the layout.

SUPPLIES *Patterned papers:* American Crafts and Chatterbox; *Metal tags:* Creative Imaginations; *Metal letters and quote sticker:* Making Memories; *Chipboard photo corners and phrases:* Heidi Swapp for Advantus; *Tacks:* Chatterbox; *Computer font:* Book Antiqua, Microsoft Word.

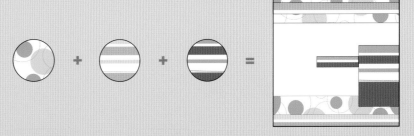

A Swedish flag of blueberry and vanilla ice cream. Of course, I had to have it. Who can resist patriotic dessert on a stick?

YELLOW AND BLUE BY ANNIE WEIS

why this works: Annie's page has great flow from top to bottom. The strips of paper (brought together beautifully with their shared colors) create stepping stones that move the eye right to her daughter's face in the bottom photo.

SUPPLIES *Patterned papers:* My Mind's Eye, Autumn Leaves and Scenic Route Paper Co.; *Stickers:* Memories Complete and Doodlebug Design; *Rub-ons and frames:* Scrapworks; *Ribbon:* Scenic Route Paper Co.; *Pen:* Zig Writer, EK Success; *Computer fonts:* Blue Highway Linocut, Bones Bummer, History Brush, Sexton Serif, Sveningsson and TagsXtreme, downloaded from the Internet.

GOTTA LOVE BY ALI EDWARDS

why this works: Matching up the same circle pattern in different color combinations creates a seamless pattern foundation. I arranged my photos to leave a pathway for journaling and a title.

additional idea: Think about the photos you take. Get close. Move far away. Tell the complete story by adding variety to your photos.

SUPPLIES *Textured cardstock:* Bazzill Basics Paper; *Patterned papers:* KI Memories; *Rub-on text:* 7gypsies; *Rub-on letters:* KI Memories, Doodlebug Design and Making Memories; *Rub-on stitching:* Autumn Leaves.

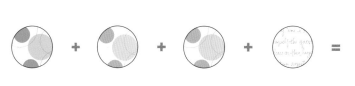

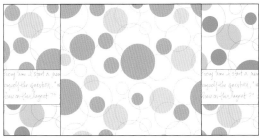

There are so many words, day to day, that I should say to you. Some that I say and wish I hadn't. But the most important, and the ones I should tell you a million times...

i lOve yoU so much.

kSA

enduring (en·door´·in) 1. lasting; permanent 2. continuing on until the end

WORDS BY JAMIE WATERS

why this works: Jamie selected patterns with a similar "feel" to help communicate her story—she chose a monochromatic color palette and four patterns with a feminine (isn't it cool that blues can be feminine?), whimsical, youthful air. Another thing I love about this layout is that the blocks of patterns aren't perfectly shaped. The different dimensions add to the overall feel of the page.

SUPPLIES *Patterned papers:* KI Memories, Autumn Leaves and SEI; *Ribbon and pen:* American Crafts; *Ribbon buckle and definition sticker:* Making Memories; *Acrylic frame, die cuts and rub-ons:* KI Memories.

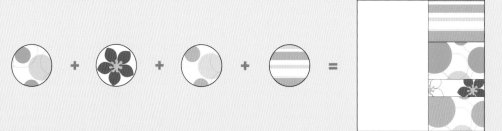

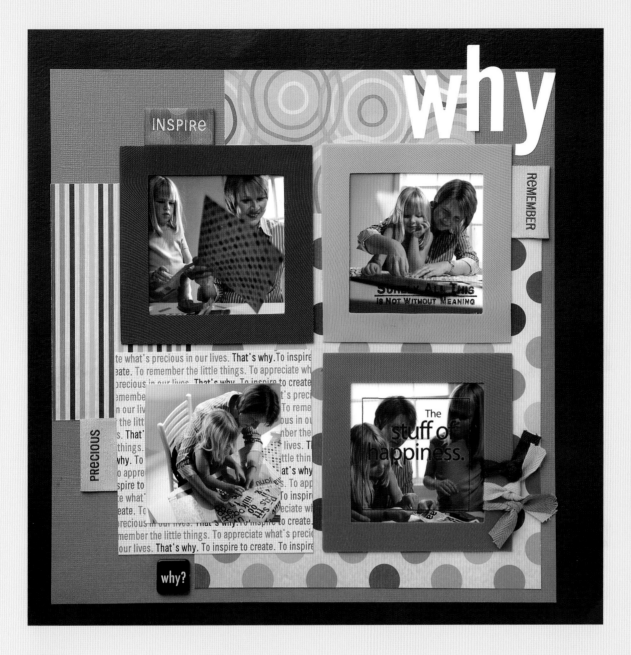

WHY BY ANNIE WEIS. PHOTOS BY PAUL KURODA, OAKLAND, CA.

why this works: Annie utilized color to unify her patterns. Decide you're going to use green and then select patterns that feature a bit of green (or a lot). Remember, it's okay if the greens aren't exactly the same! Another way to bring your layout together is to create your own text pattern, which showcases colors from each of the patterns. I love how Annie did just that on this layout.

SUPPLIES *Textured cardstock:* Bazzill Basics Paper; *Patterned papers:* Scenic Route Paper Co. and KI Memories; *Stickers:* American Crafts; *Rubber stamp:* L. Jackson, Berkeley; *Stamping ink:* ColorBox, Clearsnap; *Rub-ons:* Memories Complete; *Ribbon:* Scenic Route Paper Co.; *Tabs:* Scrapworks; *Acetate accent:* KI Memories; *Computer font:* Channel, downloaded from the Internet.

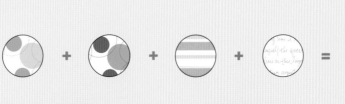

A BOY BY ALI EDWARDS

why this works: Sometimes all a layout needs is one lovely sheet of patterned paper. I love this textured patterned paper. It feels young and fresh and full of life, the perfect complement to the story. I added just a bit of green-striped ribbon for variety.

SUPPLIES *Textured cardstock:* Bazzill Basics Paper; *Patterned paper:* Paper Source; *Ribbon:* Scrapworks; *Rub-ons and quote sticker:* KI Memories; *Pen:* American Crafts; *Other:* Yellow flowers cut from ribbon.

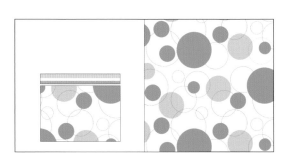

GRANDMA MARGARET BY VANESSA REYES

why this works: One of the main reasons this page works is that the combination of patterns really communicates an emotion. The photos work well with the patterns and accents, creating a feeling of joy. I see smiles and flowers and bright colors that all help tell Vanessa's story about her mother.

SUPPLIES *Patterned papers:* Marcella by K, Li'l Davis Designs and My Mind's Eye; *Fabric letter, woven tag, woven corner and snaps:* Making Memories; *Square concho and "Laughter" sticker:* Scrapworks; *Metal plate:* American Crafts; *Wooden "M":* Li'l Davis Designs; *Acrylic pebble:* Paper Studio; *Definition and tab:* Autumn Leaves; *Ribbon:* May Arts; *Other:* Flowers and metal sheet.

designer insight

I asked the contributors to this book for their best tips for choosing and using patterned papers on their layouts. Here's what Annie shared with me:

ANNIE WEIS

1. *"No method" can be a good method.* Sometimes I use lots of patterned paper, sometimes just a little. My strength as a scrapper is my versatility—I like to use everything from slivers of patterned paper to complex layers of large blocks. I don't like to get stuck in a rut, and I've found that by varying the amount of patterned paper I use, I can keep my style fresh and eclectic.

2. *Mix up the manufacturers.* I usually use papers from 2–4 manufacturers on each page. I like to choose papers that don't seem like an obvious combination; for example, I'll mix vintage, shabby and graphic together. When I notice that I use certain papers together too often, I'll ask my friends to suggest different manufacturers.

3. *Find patterns in your photos.* I always look for color combinations in my photos, but I can also often find patterns there as well. For example, you might find a floral pattern in a garden or within the print of your daughter's dress. Find papers that highlight the patterns in your photos and bring out the details that might otherwise be missed on your pages.

4. *Add emotion.* Throw in a few strips of contrasting colors and patterns for emotional impact. For example, I added a strip of red floral paper to a green-blue-and-brown masculine page to add just a touch of angry emotion to the design.

WE ARRIVE IN SANTA BARBARA ● GO FOR LUNCH AT SHORELINE CAFE ● EATING SHARK BURRITOS AND DRINKING WINE ● OUR CHAIRS SIT RIGHT IN THE SAND ● WATCHING THE GIRLS DIG IN THE SAND NEXT TO OUR TABLE ● HANGING OUT AT THE BEACH ALL AFTERNOON TEMPERATURE IS JUST RIGHT ● NOTHING MORE RELAXING ● THIS IS HEAVEN ON EARTH

SHORELINE BY ANNIE WEIS

why this works: Contrasting a very vivid block of circle-patterned paper with a stark-white background creates a cool, fresh result. The two patterned-paper blocks along the bottom serve as "legs," creating a structure and holding up the photo. Also, notice how the curved lines in the patterned paper in the lower right sweep the eye right into the title. Awesome use of pattern as a design aid.

SUPPLIES *Textured cardstock:* Bazzill Basics Paper; *Patterned papers, tabs and studs:* Scrapworks; *Epoxy stickers and rub-ons:* MOD, Autumn Leaves; *Computer font:* 2Peas Tasklist, downloaded from *www.twopeasinabucket.com.*

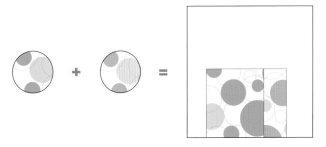

HAPPY LOVE BY JAMIE WATERS

why this works: This layout truly communicates a sense of delightful happiness. The photo, layered on top of a large circle-patterned block, combined with the floral, text and stripe patterns mesh together through color, radiating a light, bright atmosphere.

SUPPLIES *Patterned papers:* KI Memories and Li'l Davis Designs; *Tag die cuts:* KI Memories; *Epoxy letters and label sticker:* Li'l Davis Designs; *Ribbon:* Scrapworks; *Definition sticker and brad:* Making Memories; *Pen:* American Crafts.

FINDING HIS WAY BY ANNIE WEIS

why this works: When bringing a variety of patterns together, layering additional elements on top holds everything together. Here, Annie did just that by adding three circle accents directly on top of the main foundation: two punched patterned circles (that run off the edge) and one rub-on circle that connects the photo and the main circle-patterned paper.

SUPPLIES *Textured cardstock:* Bazzill Basics Paper; *Patterned papers:* BasicGrey, Scenic Route Paper Co. and 7gypsies; *Stickers:* Memories Complete and Scrapworks; *Rub-ons:* Memories Complete; *Circle punch:* EK Success; *Computer font:* American Typewriter, downloaded from the Internet; *Other:* Map stationery.

SEEK BY JAMIE WATERS

why this works: Jamie tied four different patterns together by using each as a frame for a photo. I love how she repeated the circles in the patterned papers with two perfectly placed brads on each side of the title. This layout is a terrific example of using just a bit of pattern to tell your story.

SUPPLIES *Patterned papers:* American Crafts, Scrapworks and KI Memories; *Letter stickers:* Doodlebug Design; *Tab:* Kopp Design; *Brads and pen:* American Crafts.

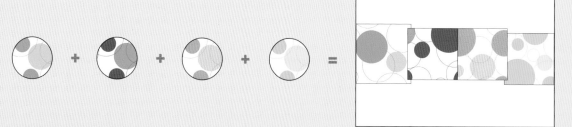

SWEET BY MILEY JOHNSON

why this works: Curves are a great complement to circle-patterned paper—especially when they bring patterns together that feature other elements (such as geometric shapes and text). You can create curves like this by freehand-cutting them or by using a paper cutter that makes curves. Create balance on a two-page layout by adding curves to both pages.

SUPPLIES *Patterned papers:* 7gypsies and Chatterbox; *Fabric letters:* Making Memories; *Vintage buttons:* Urban Art; *Chipboard letters:* Li'l Davis Designs; *Ribbon:* May Arts; *Computer font:* AL Songwriter, downloaded from www.twopeasinabucket.com.

 + + + =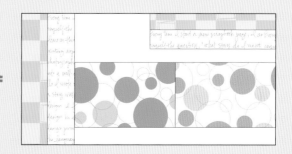

ESCAPE BY JAMIE WATERS

why this works: Jamie created balance on this layout by reflecting the gathering of elements (photo + patterned paper + rub-on words) on both the top and bottom of the page. She linked the journaling and the photos together by repeating the patterned strips in close proximity to each of the elements and layering two round brads on top.

SUPPLIES *Patterned papers:* Scrapworks and Daisy D's Paper Co.; *Rub-ons and brads:* Making Memories.

Here it is in pink, green and yellow. I have finally become Americanized. I've always insisted that a real birthday cake must be made from scratch: a sponge cake decorated with whipped cream and strawberries. And now look at this picture. For Jessie's 6th birthday cupcakes, I used only the finest artificial ingredients: white cake mix, canned frosting, neon food coloring, and multi-colored sprinkles. The Kindergarten kids were wildly enthusiastic, of course. And, I admit it, so was I. Yep, I'm officially American now. Cupcake, anyone??

PROOF BY ANNIE WEIS

why this works: Circles everywhere! Mix a photo filled with circles with circle-patterned paper for a cohesive, fun layout. I love the contrast Annie brought into the design by placing a long, rectangular journaling block right across the patterned strips and on top of the photo. It perfectly links the long strips to the large photo.

SUPPLIES *Patterned papers:* KI Memories, Scrapworks and BasicGrey; *Stickers:* American Crafts; *Concho and frame:* Scrapworks; *Computer font:* Futura Book, downloaded from *www.myfonts.com*.

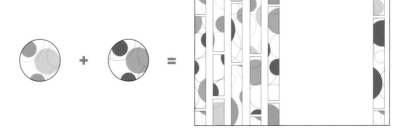

BIKE PHOTOS BY ALI EDWARDS

why this works: I punched small circles of dense patterns and paired them with lighter patterns for a balanced look. Repeating the punched circles on both pages and connecting them with a hand-drawn line brings your eye from one group of circles to the next. I also connected both pages of the spread by layering an element that spans both pages.

additional idea: I love patterns I can write on and still have legible journaling. Try it!

SUPPLIES *Textured cardstock:* Bazzill Basics Paper; *Patterned papers:* Scrapworks (stripes), Anna Griffin (circle, floral), Paper Source (floral); *Rub-ons:* Making Memories (white) and 7gypsies (black); *Circle punch:* Punch Bunch; *Silver circle accent:* Maya Road; *Pen:* American Crafts; *Photo corners:* Two Peas in a Bucket; *Other:* Card.

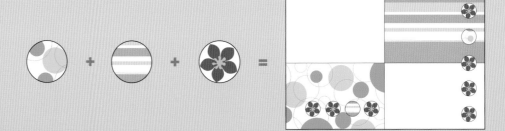

The Cutest LITTLE

big temper

Well . . . I'm pretty sure you're gonna be mad at me for this one when you grow up, but I just couldn't help myself! You started doing this crazy hysterical

SCReAM . . aaaahh

at about 5 ½ months. At first I was scared, thought maybe you had hurt yourself, but I caught on pretty quick . . . I think our tempers are too much alike maybe even identical. Now that you are almost 8 months you are still doing your famous scream, and now I hate to admit it, but I just can't help but laugh (just a little) right before I pick you up and sooth all your worries. You are definitely my son, and I'm seeing so much of myself in you already. 8/05

¡bada bing!

THE CUTEST LITTLE BIG TEMPER BY VANESSA REYES

why this works: On this page, Vanessa successfully balanced the large photo block on the left with the pattern + photo block on the right. To bring the two together, she overlapped the title from the left to the right, avoiding a "hard" line separation between the two sides. She also added wonderful little circle accents—the clear buttons and the circle tag—that repeat the patterns on the right.

SUPPLIES *Patterned papers:* American Crafts; *Rub-ons and metal letters:* KI Memories; *Photo corner and small flower:* Chatterbox; *Acetate letters:* Heidi Swapp for Advantus; *Letter stickers:* American Crafts and Heidi Grace Designs; *Clear buttons:* foof-a-La, Autumn Leaves; *Clear heart:* Heidi Grace Designs; *Button:* Making Memories; *Circle sticker:* Christina Cole for Provo Craft; *Ribbon:* May Arts; *Other:* White brads.

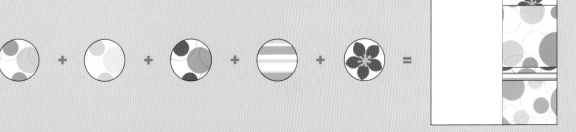

ZOO BY ANNIE WEIS

why this works: Annie used patterns to create homes for her journaling and embellishments. The colorful patterned vellum overlaid on top of the foundation creates a nice contrast with the black-and-white stripes of the zebra and complements the colors in the photo.

SUPPLIES *Textured cardstock:* Prism Papers; *Patterned papers:* Chatterbox and KI Memories; *Vellum:* American Crafts; *Rub-ons:* Colorbök; *Buttons:* Magic Scraps; *Computer font:* Bones Bummer, downloaded from the Internet; *Other:* Staples.

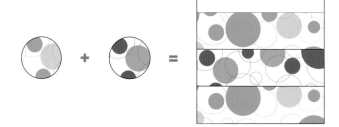

SHE GOT HER EARS PIERCED BY MILEY JOHNSON

why this works: The circle patterns evoke the idea of earrings (notice how Miley also used jeweled brads in bright colors) and give this page an energetic feel that communicates a young girl's excitement about getting her ears pierced. Also, the patterned papers repeat the colors in Miley's photographs (the brightly colored shopping bag and the stripes on her daughter's sweater).

SUPPLIES *Patterned papers:* BasicGrey, KI Memories and Christina Cole for Provo Craft; *Felt flowers:* Paper Source; *Plastic letters:* Heidi Swapp for Advantus; *Rhinestone brads:* SEI; *Letter stickers:* Making Memories; *Computer font:* 2Peas Red Velvet Cake, downloaded from *www.twopeasinabucket.com; Other:* Shopping bag.

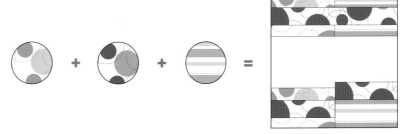

RACHAEL AND NICK BY JAMIE WATERS

why this works: The patterns divide the page into visual spaces where your eyes can rest before returning to the focal-point photo. The soft matching hues of the patterned papers work together to create a vision of two lives unified in a successful marriage.

SUPPLIES *Patterned papers and die cuts:* KI Memories; *Rub-ons:* Autumn Leaves; *Buttons:* SEI.

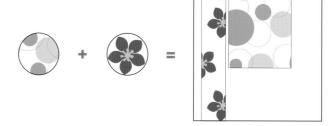

chapter summary

CHAPTER 1: CIRCLES

1. *Create unity on your page by repeating a variety of circle patterns.*

2. *Position accents inside of circles—and don't be afraid to allow elements to overlap the edges of circles.*

3. *Look for circle elements within your photographs (a baseball, an earring) and repeat them on your page.*

4. *Use circles like stepping stones to direct the eye to your focal-point photo.*

5. *Match up the same circle pattern in different color combinations for an eye-catching page background or border.*

6. *Contrast a bright circle-patterned paper with a stark-white background for a cool, fresh result.*

7. *Layer circle patterns on top of each other to add dimension to your layout.*

Some days *just* ROCK.

All together for a weekend. The nicest place. Summer 2005 camping with friends in Ashland • gotta love friends, like Jason, who are skilled with a camera. I love these photos because they are real. Ha ha ha. Because we are laughing. And being silly. Just being us.

Look at the trees, look at the birds ... and you will be able to see that the whole existence is joyful. Everything is simply happy. Trees are happy for no reason; they are not going to become prime ministers or presidents and they will never have any bank balance. Look at the flowers — for no reason. It is simply unbelievable how happy flowers are.

Osho

florals

PATTERNED PAPER

My parents live and breathe gardening, so flowers have always been a part of my life. I grew up in a home overflowing with fresh flowers. And walking into our backyard? It was like walking into another world full of color, texture and variety. Talk about a cool way to be introduced to nature's awesome sense of design!

No matter what the season, flowers are a *part of our lives*. Take a moment and look around your space. Where do you see flowers? I see flowers almost everywhere I look: on a book jacket, in a piece of art, on a piece of fabric. Is it any wonder we send flowers as gifts to celebrate new life, to cheer someone up, to bring a smile to someone's face, to offer condolences?

Flowers have their own sense of *energy and life*. They evoke memories (of Grandmother's wallpaper or the sweet little dress you wore as a child) and symbolize celebrations (think of a wedding bouquet, a homecoming corsage, a red rose to celebrate enduring love on an anniversary). A flower garden can be a peaceful sanctuary or a place to party.

SOME DAYS JUST ROCK BY ALI EDWARDS

SUPPLIES ON OPPOSITE PAGE *Textured cardstock:* Bazzill Basics Paper; *Patterned papers:* Scenic Route Paper Co. (large floral) and Pressed Petals (small floral); *Rub-ons:* KI Memories (green flower and text) and Creative Imaginations; *Small phrase stickers:* K&Company; *Large brads:* Making Memories; *Transparency:* 3M.

Take a moment and think about how flowers have helped define the moments in your life. Think of the flowers that surrounded you as a child, of the first flower you received from someone who loved you, of your favorite flowers. Note the different emotions those flowers evoke. Now, think about the ways you can use these emotions to help tell a story on a scrapbook page.

In art and in our scrapbooks, flowers can convey all kinds of emotions. Floral-patterned papers can be an important part of sharing a message or telling a story. Here are a few of the messages I think floral prints help communicate. Revise this list, add to it, make it your own.

- CELEBRATION
- HAPPINESS
- FEMININITY
- PEACE
- GARDEN
- GROWTH
- VARIETY
- JOY
- CEREMONY
- UPLIFTING
- BEAUTY
- LIFE

Choose floral prints because you love them and because of the stories they can help you tell on your pages. In this chapter, I'll show you how.

U EAT BY ALI EDWARDS

why this works: Light floral patterns are perfect for background papers. On this layout, the floral motifs **soften** the overall design, **balancing** out the hard lines in the photos and on the striped ribbon. Soft floral patterns also make excellent homes for computer-generated or handwritten journaling.

SUPPLIES *Textured cardstock:* Bazzill Basics Paper; *Patterned papers:* Scrapworks (stripes); Pressed Petals (floral); foof-a-La (floral), Autumn Leaves; *Rub-on letters:* Making Memories; *Circle accent:* Rhonna Farrer, Autumn Leaves.

 + + =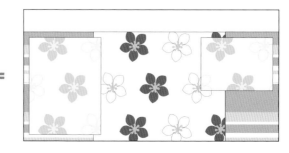

be original be alive be grateful

USA

American Girl

You love pop music, bubble gum and of course apple pie! There really is no denying that you are the poster child of what an American girl represents. I see a spunk in you that I know is partially due to the way you are able to express yourself, and how we are able to raise you as an American. Even at the young age of four, you know what patriotism is, and know that it is important to love your country and the service men and women who protect and keep our freedom safe. You knew the pledge of allegiance before you even knew how to write your name, and the star spangled banner and the grand old flag are two of your favorite songs. You know that if you want to pray at a restaurant, you can, and no one will tell you otherwise. You know that the flag stands for freedom. You are the complete American package. Proud, independent and free to be the person you want to become..there are no boundaries to what you can do, you are an American..living the American dream.

choose joy

B free

AMERICAN GIRL BY MILEY JOHNSON

why this works: Miley **unified** the patterns on her layout by picking two colors from her photo and choosing patterns based on those colors. Remember that matching is a relative term—go for a pattern that evokes the feelings you want to communicate on your layout. Balance out the two vivid patterns with a canvas of white cardstock as a foundation for your photo and journaling.

SUPPLIES *Patterned papers, stencils, tacks, rub-ons, chipboard letters and ribbon:* Chatterbox; *Star punch:* Family Treasures; *Staples:* Making Memories.

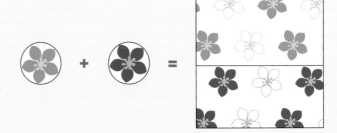

FIRST LIBRARY VISIT BY VANESSA REYES

why this works: Here, three smaller patterned strips complement one large floral pattern. I love how Vanessa directly connected the background floral pattern with the photo by **overlapping** a large stamp and a wood frame. She also added two photo corners on opposite edges to keep the eye within the layout. The feeling is very soft and feminine.

SUPPLIES *Patterned paper, wood frame, wood tag, photo corner, chipboard letter, ribbon and die cut:* Chatterbox; *Label sticker:* Li'l Davis Designs; *Foam stamps, acrylic paint and crystal brad:* Making Memories; *Letter stamps:* Educational Insights; *Other:* Metal sheet.

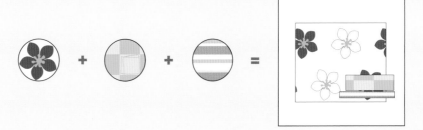

SUN KISSED BY MILEY JOHNSON

why this works: I love how Miley added **white space** in the form of the pink cardstock. Removing some of the background pattern allowed her to add large plastic flowers without overwhelming the photos. The flower accents also bring out the floral pattern in the paper.

SUPPLIES *Patterned papers:* Chatterbox and Rusty Pickle; *Chipboard letter:* Heidi Swapp for Advantus; *Nails and patterned chipboard letters:* Chatterbox; *Ribbon:* Hobby Lobby; *Clay letters:* Li'l Davis Designs; *Flower punch:* Family Treasures; *Computer font:* CBX Watson, "Journaling Fonts" CD, Chatterbox.

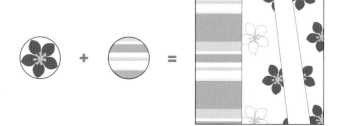

FAMILY BY VANESSA REYES

why this works: Vanessa paired a small, **tight** floral pattern with a loose floral pattern (notice how they share a similar green color—good for consistency) to create an overall balance between the two.

SUPPLIES *Handmade paper:* Paper Source; *Patterned papers:* Scrapworks and Petals & Possibilities; *Letter stickers:* Chatterbox and Mustard Moon; *Canvas frame and brads:* Making Memories; *Ribbon:* May Arts and Li'l Davis Designs; *Other:* Vintage trim.

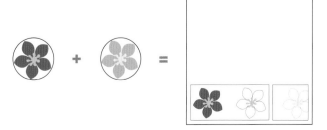

designer insight

I asked the contributors to my book for their best tips for choosing and using patterned paper on their layouts. Here's what Vanessa shared with me:

VANESSA REYES

1. *Choose patterns you love!* I love floral prints in almost any color, shape, size and pattern. You'll see floral prints all over my scrapbook pages; it's easy to spot my personal style in my albums. Use what you love—as much of it as you like!

2. *Use black-and-white photographs.* I love color photographs, but I also love how a black-and-white photo really stands out against a colorful background. A black-and-white photo can be simply beautiful. Try converting your photos to sepia tones for interesting effects as well.

3. *Scrapbook inside of a line—or outside of one.* If you're just getting started with patterned paper, it's easy to mix and match patterns by choosing two different prints from one manufacturer. The manufacturer has done the hard work for you because the color and the style and maybe even the scale of the print have all been designed to work together. Don't make it harder than it has to be.

4. *Play with placement.* I use patterned paper for all sorts of things. I use it to mat photographs. I'll use it as part of a title. I like to cut accents out of it. I'll use it to cover tags. I'll sometimes even write my journaling directly on it. There are hundreds of ways to play with patterned paper on a page—have fun discovering where you want to put yours!

BEAUTIFUL MIRACLE BY VANESSA REYES

why this works: This combination of patterns works because the patterns **create** a feeling of softness, of love and innocence. The dark cardstock provides a lovely contrast to the gathering of light papers, embellishments and the photo (as well as a resting spot for the viewer's eye).

SUPPLIES *Textured cardstock:* Bazzill Basics Paper; *Patterned papers:* Autumn Leaves; *Transparency:* K&Company; *Chipboard letters:* Heidi Swapp for Advantus; *Tags:* K&Company; *Paper flower:* Prima; *Rub-ons:* BasicGrey; *Word strip:* Christina Cole for Provo Craft; *Staples and crystal brad:* Making Memories; *Ribbon:* May Arts; *Border and tag stickers:* Scrapworks; *Letter stickers:* American Crafts; *Letter stamps:* 7gypsies; *Stamping ink:* ColorBox, Clearsnap.

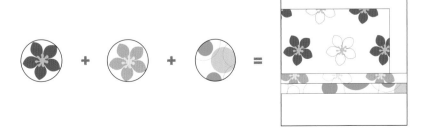

HAPPY BIRTHDAY TO YOU BY ALI EDWARDS

why this works: I love when I complete a page that just feels seamless, when the photos, the patterns and the accents all work together in **harmony**. For this layout, I wanted the patterns to simply blend and support the photos and the story. I chose unobtrusive patterns—a classic black-and-white, and a light-green floral. Each feels modern, yet they're soft enough to take a backseat to the photos.

SUPPLIES *Textured cardstock:* Bazzill Basics Paper; *Patterned papers:* Chatterbox and Scrapworks; *Rub-on stitching:* Autumn Leaves; *Computer font:* Adler, downloaded from the Internet; *Ribbon:* American Crafts.

[inner] BEAUTY

You are blessed with the gift of exceptional beauty, but it's who you are on the inside that makes you so special to me. Don't compare yourself to others, because no one else could ever take your place. I hope that someday you will realize the value of inner beauty...because you are beautiful inside and out.

INNER BEAUTY BY ANNIE WEIS

why this works: The **repetition** of the large circle shapes makes this a totally cool and visually pleasing page. The patterns support the theme of beauty and complement the silliness captured in the photos. The overlapped, hard-edged text block is a nice contrast to the circles. Also, notice how the three flower leaf points (a great **visual triangle** of accents) bring the eye into the journaling.

SUPPLIES *Textured cardstock:* Bazzill Basics Paper; *Patterned papers:* Anna Griffin, K&Company, 7gypsies, Scenic Route Paper Co., Scrapworks and My Mind's Eye; *Rub-ons:* Phrase Café, EK Success; *Circle punch:* Marvy Uchida; *Stamping ink:* ColorBox, Clearsnap; *Die cuts:* Scrapworks; *Canvas flowers:* foof-a-La, Autumn Leaves; *Leather flower and decorative brad:* Making Memories; *Paper flower:* Prima; *Other:* Silk flowers and brads.

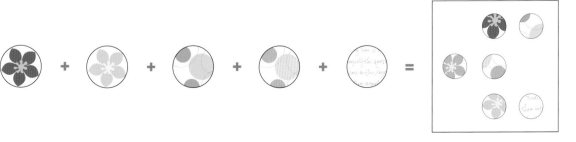

LOVE JK BY MILEY JOHNSON

why this works: Creating additional accents that **repeat** the patterns is a great way to add harmony to a layout. Here, the hearts made from patterned strips (in conjunction with the stitched tails and flower accents) bring you from one page into the next.

SUPPLIES *Patterned papers:* KI Memories, 7gypsies, Die Cuts With a View and Anna Griffin; *Iron-ons, foam stamps and acrylic paint:* Heidi Swapp for Advantus; *Metal words:* All My Memories; *Paper flowers:* Prima; *Buttons:* Junkitz; *Computer font:* AL Outdoors, downloaded from *www.twopeasinabucket.com.*

 + + + =

INTERESTING PLACES BY ALI EDWARDS

why this works: When I work with patterned papers, I often cut them into geometric shapes, especially squares, rectangles and circles. Reducing the size of the patterns seems to make them more manageable. From there I bring all of the pieces back together into a **grid format**. After I've laid out the grid, I layer additional accents over the top to link the separate pieces together visually—not all of them, of course, but enough so my eye sees the relationship between the smaller pieces.

additional idea: See the patterns in your world. See the blades of grass. See the oranges heaped together at the outdoor market. See the wood chips that make up the ground cover on the playground. Bring those patterns into your scrapbooking.

SUPPLIES *Textured cardstock:* Bazzill Basics Paper; *Patterned papers:* Chatterbox (floral); Wild Asparagus (stripes), My Mind's Eye; 7gypsies (circles); *Circle accents:* Memories Complete and Chatterbox; *Word stickers:* 7gypsies and Wordsworth.

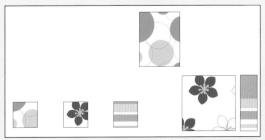

HOW *beautiful* IS YOUTH! HOW BRIGHT IT GLEAMS,
WITH ITS' ILLUSIONS, *aspirations*, DREAM!
BOOK OF *beginnings*, STORY WITHOUT END,
EACH MAID A HEROINE, AND EACH MAN *a friend!*
HENRY WADSWORTH LONGFELLOW

follow your dreams

lovely

daughter

enjoy

a happy heart makes the face cheerful. PROVERBS 15:13

FOLLOW YOUR DREAMS BY VANESSA REYES

why this works: Here, Vanessa combined a large floral pattern with two smaller patterns that have a similar shade of blue (I love how it's very faint in the yellow pattern). The space between each of the pattern blocks **visually separates** them, adding a more concrete structure to the layout.

SUPPLIES *Patterned papers and buttons:* foof-a-La, Autumn Leaves; *Bookplate, fabric pocket, metal-rimmed tags and metal frame:* Making Memories; *Chipboard heart:* Heidi Swapp for Advantus; *Epoxy letter:* Marcela by K; *Metal plates:* American Crafts; *Ribbon:* May Arts; *Clear stickers:* Autumn Leaves; *Transparency:* Die Cuts With a View; *Other:* Twill tape.

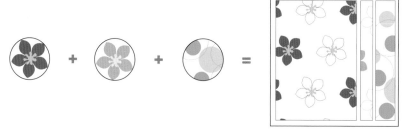

4 GET ME NOT BY MILEY JOHNSON

why this works: Miley found the perfect floral pattern to use with her photos of forget-me-nots. Plus, the striped paper perfectly coordinates with her floral print. Notice how she even incorporated the forget-me-not theme into her page title.

SUPPLIES *Patterned papers, tacks, ribbon and frames:* Chatterbox; *Tags:* Avery; *Twill:* Hobby Lobby.

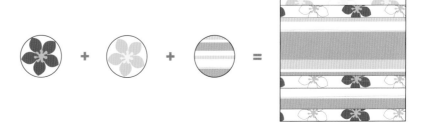

JULY 4TH BY VANESSA REYES

why this works: I love that Vanessa didn't choose patterned papers that showcase fireworks, nor did she go all out with the red, white and blue for this page. Instead, she went with feeling. She brought two different floral patterns together (as well as a circle pattern, nicely complemented by the button accents) that spoke to her and helped tell the story she wanted to **communicate** about her memories.

SUPPLIES *Patterned papers:* Chatterbox, Rusty Pickle, American Crafts, Petals & Possibilities and Autumn Leaves; *Clear letter sticker:* Autumn Leaves; *Chipboard letter:* Heidi Swapp for Advantus; *Metal letter:* Making Memories; *Wooden "4":* Li'l Davis Designs; *Ribbon:* May Arts and Li'l Davis Designs; *Number stamps:* PSX Design; *Stamping ink:* ColorBox, Clearsnap; *Other:* Vintage trim.

SILLY US BY ALI EDWARDS

why this works: For this layout, I cut three pieces of patterned paper into squares and rectangles, and adhered them to a background sheet of cardstock. The cream border around the photos keeps the **focus** on them, and the green rub-on letters **complement** the patterns, bringing the green color forward within the design.

SUPPLIES *Patterned papers:* Chatterbox (floral), Imagination Project (floral) and KI Memories (text); *Rub-on letters:* Scrapworks; *Oval tag:* KI Memories; *Round tag:* EK Success; *Ribbon:* May Arts; *Stamping ink:* ColorBox Fluid Chalk, Clearsnap; *Smiley face stamp:* Technique Tuesday; *Pen:* American Crafts.

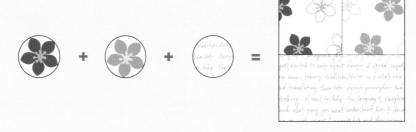

1ST DAY OF SCHOOL BY VANESSA REYES

why this works: A tightly cropped photo of a face is a great **complement** to the thin strips of floral paper Vanessa gathered on the left side. Also, notice how she created a cool frame for her title. The frame separates the title from the patterns and focuses the viewer's attention on the title area.

SUPPLIES *Patterned papers:* Chatterbox; *Metal-rimmed tags and definition sticker:* Making Memories; *Chipboard number:* Heidi Swapp for Advantus; *Clear clip:* Autumn Leaves; *Pencil sticker:* EK Success; *Letter stickers:* K&Company, Heidi Grace Designs and Making Memories; *Flower sticker:* Colorbök; *Acrylic accent:* KI Memories.

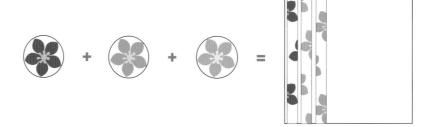

"I am a dreamer because I have a lot of dreams."

"Some I have already accomplished."

—from a 5th grade essay by Kira 9-2005

never stop dreaming, babe

dreamy

DREAMS BY JAMIE WATERS

why this works: The one large piece of floral-patterned paper creates a great home for Jamie's photo and accents. The large section of blue cardstock **balances** the complexity within the pattern. Jamie also created a nice **visual triangle** with the two white quote strips on the top, the photo and the round "Dreamy" accent.

SUPPLIES *Patterned papers and pillow accent:* Autumn Leaves; *Canvas tag, bookplate, ribbon and stitching embellishments:* Li'l Davis Designs; *Typewriter "K":* Two Peas in a Bucket; *Transparency:* Narratives, Creative Imaginations; *Brads:* American Crafts; *Computer font:* 2Peas A Little Loopy, downloaded from *www.twopeasinabucket.com*.

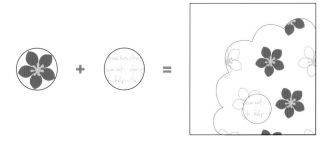

GLIMPSES 2004 BY ALI EDWARDS

why this works: I selected a single sheet of patterned paper as a secondary frame (the first frame is the foundation cardstock) and used a color from the pattern as the jumping-off point for my additional accents, stamping ink, etc. Notice how the large "S" on the red tag **links** the photo block with the journaling below. *Tip:* I punched squares out of the tabbed file cards and placed my photos behind them.

SUPPLIES *Textured cardstock:* Bazzill Basics Paper; *Patterned papers:* foof-a-La (floral), Autumn Leaves; *Making Memories (stripes); Square accents with tabs and rub-on letters:* Autumn Leaves; *Fabric tag:* Art Warehouse, Creative Imaginations; *"S":* BasicGrey; *"U" stamp:* Heidi Swapp for Advantus; *Stamping ink:* Ranger Industries.

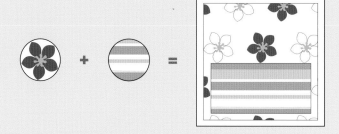

FOR YOU 05 BY VANESSA REYES

why this works: The floral patterns on this layout speak of beauty and love, and they harmonize because of their softness. Tie a variety of floral patterns together by choosing papers with a similar **feeling** or mood. Sound technical enough? This is part of the main idea: choosing patterns is personal. And I love that! Ask yourself how the patterns make you feel rather than worrying if the pinks match exactly.

SUPPLIES *Textured cardstock:* Bazzill Basics Paper; *Patterned papers:* Chatterbox and Autumn Leaves; *Stitched tag and letter stickers:* Chatterbox; *Envelope:* Creative Imaginations; *Tab:* Autumn Leaves; *Printed twill and letter-sticker strip:* 7gypsies; *Blue rub-ons:* KI Memories; *Transparency quote:* Die Cuts With a View; *Number stamps:* PSX Design; *Stamping ink:* ColorBox, Clearsnap; *Metal plate:* American Crafts.

Difficult things take a long time, impossible things a little longer.

Obstacles are those frightful things you see when you take your eyes off your goal.
-Henry Ford

When the world says, "Give up," Hope whispers, "Try it one more time."
-unknown

DON'T BE DISCOURAGED. IT'S OFTEN THE LAST KEY IN THE BUNCH THAT OPENS THE LOCK.
-UNKNOWN

TRY

I know it's hard. It's just too much.
You think you can't do it.
You're so tired.

Don't cry, my girl. Don't give up. Don't quit.

You can do it. I believe in you.

don't quit

TRY BY ANNIE WEIS

why this works: **Intermixing** the floral strips with the quotes helps unify the colors in the quotes with the colors in the photo. The variation in the length of the strips and quotes make them great **directional tools**, leading the eye back to the main photo.

SUPPLIES *Patterned papers:* BasicGrey and KI Memories; *Letter stickers:* Scrapworks; *Clear rubber stamps:* Technique Tuesday; *Stamping ink:* ColorBox, Clearsnap; *Buttons:* 7gypsies; *Gem fastener:* Magic Scraps; *Computer font:* Sveningsson, downloaded from the Internet.

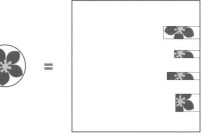

chapter summary

CHAPTER 2: FLORALS

1. *Create a beautiful page background with a single sheet of pretty floral paper.*

2. *Write your journaling directly on top of a soft floral print.*

3. *Balance two vivid floral patterns with white cardstock as a page background.*

4. *Pair a small, tight floral pattern with a loose floral pattern to create a balanced look on your page.*

5. *Combine floral patterns successfully by starting with prints that feature a similar feeling or mood.*

6. *Soften straight lines on your layout with a subtle floral pattern.*

7. *Bring out the florals within a pattern by adding flower accents to your page.*

Be the ART. What does this mean? It means being present. Living for today. Fully experiencing everything. Creating. Bringing what is inside... outside. playing. Being brave and open. Not worrying what others think. Love that you have been loving art play. Such a great way to grow. Growing open with art.

ESTABLISHED: summer 2005

BE THE ART

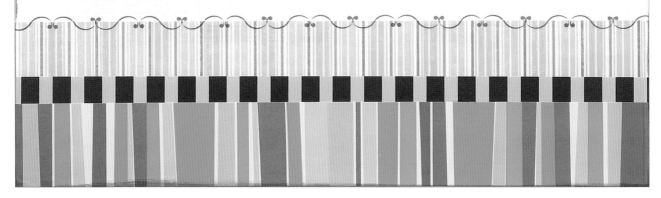

You don't have to be an artist to know there is magic in letting go and throwing down lines, letting your subconscious drive for a while. It's an ideal way to discover ideas, be playful, and quash that inner critic.

from veer.com

stripes

PATTERNED PAPER

Thinking of stripes conjures up a bunch of images for me: Simon in his PJ's from Old Navy; my favorite rainbow-striped comforter as a child (man, I loved that thing); old wood paneling; candy canes; my handsome husband, Chris, all dressed up in his pin-striped shirt; white picket fences; railroad tracks. So many things in our world are composed of a couple of lines arranged one next to the other.

Most of the time stripes are super orderly—long, evenly spaced lines that communicate stability and balance. In other instances they can be light and whimsical depending on the width and the straightness of the lines. Want to make something look taller? Use stripes vertically. Wider? Turn the paper so the stripes are running horizontally. Sometimes all you need to do to more effectively tell your story is to turn your paper 90 degrees. Seem too simple? Try it.

BE THE ART BY ALI EDWARDS

SUPPLIES ON OPPOSITE PAGE *Textured cardstock:* Bazzill Basics Paper; *Patterned papers:* Bo-Bunny Press, Magic Scraps and Cross-My-Heart; *Chipboard letters:* Heidi Swapp for Advantus; *Rub-on accent:* Fontwerks; *Rubber stamp:* 7gypsies; *Stamping ink:* Stampin' Up!; *Pens:* American Crafts.

If you're new to patterned papers, stripes are a great place to start. Begin with just a strip (with the stripes oriented vertically so you can see all the colors and/or stripes) and use it as a simple accent along the bottom of your layout—or to divide content on your page. Colorful stripes are also perfect for harmonizing a variety of colors in your photos or other accents. Remember, the key is to play. To use what you love and what you have. I'm guessing you may have a couple of sheets of striped paper just waiting to be used. Get inspired by the following pages and go for it.

Stripes often represent the following ideas in art. Revise this list, add to it, make it your own.

- DIRECTION
- MASCULINITY
- GOAL
- ENERGY

- TRADITION
- STRENGTH
- GUIDANCE
- HISTORY
- TRUST

- RELIABILITY
- MOVEMENT
- BALANCE
- NATURE

Choose striped prints because you love them and because of the stories they can help you tell on your pages. In this chapter, I'll show you how.

SWEET HARVEST BY ALI EDWARDS

why this works: I created balance on my two-page spread by pairing a 12" x 8" photo with a 12" x 8" piece of patterned paper. Remember, the colors in your patterns don't have to come from your photos. Here, I simply liked the diagonal-striped paper and wanted to use it on my layout. When mixing patterns, also consider creating accents that **repeat** the patterns used in the foundations (in this case, the rectangle accent on page one and the circle accent on page two; both include and repeat the main patterns).

SUPPLIES *Textured cardstock:* Bazzill Basics Paper; *Patterned papers:* Scenic Route Paper Co. (stripes), Li'l Davis Designs (geometric) and Making Memories (stripes); *Rub-on circle:* Memories Complete; *"E" accent:* KI Memories; *Rectangle punch:* Marvy Uchida; *Vellum:* Autumn Leaves; *Number die cuts:* QuicKutz; *Rub-on letters:* KI Memories; *Pen:* Slick Writer, American Crafts.

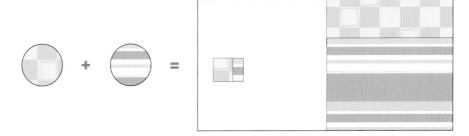

M IS FOR MISCHIEF BY MILEY JOHNSON

why this works: Bring additional attention to your focal-point photo and title by **changing the orientation** of striped patterned paper. You can achieve a completely different effect simply by switching from horizontal to vertical.

SUPPLIES *Patterned papers:* Bo-Bunny Press and Chatterbox; *Stickers:* 7gypsies; *Rubber stamps:* Hero Arts; *Stamping ink:* Tsukineko; *Metal letters:* Making Memories; *Buttons:* foof-a-La, Autumn Leaves; *Other:* Brads and wooden letters

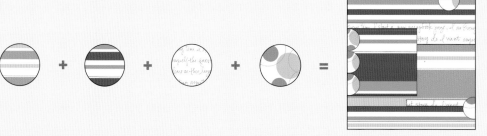

WELCOME TO OUR FAMILY BY VANESSA REYES

why this works: This layout is a great example of bringing a variety of patterns together without overwhelming the design. The secret? **Give each pattern a home.** Each of the patterns is used as part of a tag, representing each of the family members. Photos and accents cover a majority of the patterns on each tag, yet the patterns work to visually and thematically bring it all together.

SUPPLIES *Textured cardstock:* Bazzill Basics Paper; *Patterned papers, wood tags, photo corners, stickers, rub-ons and letter stickers:* Chatterbox; *Ribbon:* May Arts; *Jump ring and safety pin:* Making Memories.

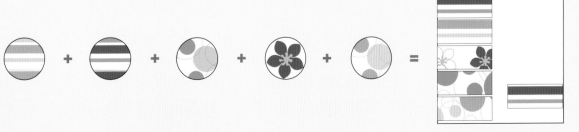

SIMON'S PRESCHOOL BY ALI EDWARDS

why this works: This layout is organized around **three main rectangles of content.** The top layer is a stripe pattern with journaling written directly on the paper; the second is a text pattern that reflects sentiments of youth; and the third is a montage of photos showing all the cool stuff Simon did at preschool. One additional layer—the title section—overlaps the top two and makes the entire design more interesting. I love organizing content into sections and then breaking out a bit from those confines to add variety and energy.

SUPPLIES *Textured cardstock:* Bazzill Basics Paper; *Patterned papers:* Sweetwater (stripes), Pebbles Inc. (text) and Li'l Davis Designs ("Cool" text); *Rub-ons:* Doodlebug Design; Dee's Designs, My Mind's Eye; *Pen:* Zig Millennium, EK Success; *Ribbon:* May Arts; *Quote and small patterned accents:* KI Memories.

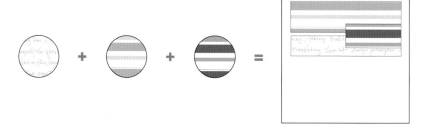

reading in mama's bed. july 2005

VERY GOOD READ

You are a book-boy. You have been since the very beginning... always up for a read or a flip through to simply check out the pictures at your own pace. You are great at identifying your favorite elements and have many memorized. just one of your special talents. Glad we can share this love of books together. So cool.

VERY GOOD READ BY ALI EDWARDS

why this works: I added **contrast** to hard lines by creating curves when cutting the patterned paper. I layered the three patterns on top of each other so the curves match from one sheet to the next. Also, I sanded the edges of each of the patterned papers (you can also sand around the edge of the layout) to create a **cohesive** effect. This can be especially effective with patterns that may not seem to go together at first.

SUPPLIES *Textured cardstock:* Bazzill Basics Paper; *Patterned papers:* Scrapworks (stripes), Chatterbox (stripes) and K&Company (floral); *Rectangle sticker:* KI Memories; *Tab and rub-on stitching:* Autumn Leaves; *Chipboard letters:* Heidi Swapp for Advantus; *Pen:* American Crafts.

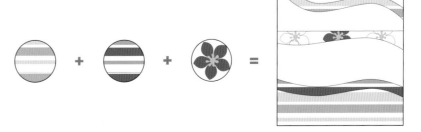

designer insight

I asked the contributors to this book for their best tips for choosing and using patterned paper on their layouts. Here's what Jamie shared with me:

JAMIE WATERS

1. *Choose the mood.* I like to look at the photograph first and then think about the story I want to tell. Then I match the mood of my story to the mood of my patterned paper. If I'm working on a happy layout, I'll choose bright colors, bold shapes, large flowers and so on. Think about what happy means to you and choose accordingly!

2. *Unity is a great common denominator.* You don't have to remember anything about fractions to know this: two different patterned papers can work together when they share something in common. A page looks unified when two patterns have a common ground, such as a common color, a common style or a common design.

3. *Portions are important to me.* I often use blocks and strips of patterned paper on my layouts. This makes it much easier for me to mix and match as many designs as I'd like. Sometimes I'll cut two pieces of patterned paper to the same proportions to create a balanced look on my page.

4. *Have fun!* It's fun to experiment with different patterns and discover a good match. It's kind of like digging through your closet and discovering a shirt that wasn't bought with a skirt—but they match!

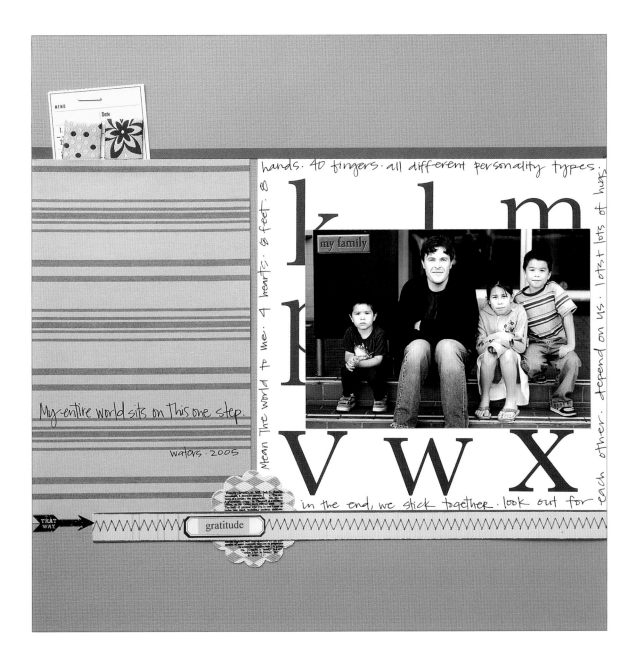

Journaling on layout: hands. 40 fingers. all different personality types. Mean the world to me. 4 hearts. 8 feet. 8 ... depend on us. lots + lots of hugs. in the end, we stick together. look out for each other.

My entire world sits on this one step.

waters . 2005

My family

THAT WAY

gratitude

MY FAMILY BY JAMIE WATERS

why this works: The strong **directional lines** on this striped patterned paper help move the eye from left to right, right into the heart of the layout. Lined patterns also make great homes for journaling, or parts of journaling, as seen here on Jamie's layout.

SUPPLIES *Patterned papers:* Li'l Davis Designs and Daisy D's Paper Co.; *Metal plaque:* Making Memories; *Tag and rub-ons:* 7gypsies; *Fabric flower:* Autumn Leaves; *Fabric tabs:* Scrapworks; *Pen:* American Crafts.

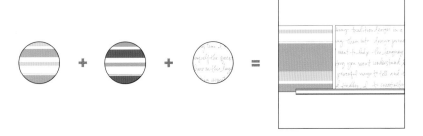

SANDBOX BY ALI EDWARDS

why this works: Sometimes you simply need to **make your own patterns**. These cool extra-large rectangle tags make a great foundation for a pattern that links the two pages together. I turned my stamp pad upside down and pressed it directly onto the page. Next, I added my favorite three-rectangle rubber stamp in a stair-step fashion, moving the eye from one page to the next. As a final touch to my pattern, I added definition stickers and rub-ons that relate to the story in my journaling.

SUPPLIES *Textured cardstock:* Bazzill Basics Paper; *Patterned papers:* Memory Box; *Rub-on stitching:* Autumn Leaves; *Large rectangle cards:* The Weathered Door; *Rub-on words, definition stickers and "S" accent:* Making Memories; *Rub-on quote:* Die Cuts With a View; *Patterned pillow accent:* MOD, Autumn Leaves; *Ribbon:* May Arts; *Rubber stamps:* Stamp It!; *Stamping ink:* ColorBox Fluid Chalk, Clearsnap; Ranger Industries.

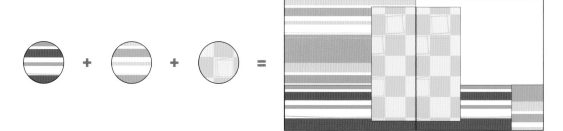

TOO FAST BY MILEY JOHNSON

why this works: Miley combined circle patterns, stripes and text for a cool foundation for her photos and additional accents. Try creating your own "striped" background on a layout by **combining and repeating** a variety of patterns and journaling strips.

SUPPLIES *Patterned papers:* SEI, 7gypsies and Provo Craft; *Chipboard circles:* Bazzill Basics Paper; *Chipboard flowers:* Making Memories; *Tiles:* Junkitz; *Rhinestone stickers and chipboard letters:* Heidi Swapp for Advantus; *Computer font:* 2Peas Red Velvet Cake, downloaded from *www.twopeasinabucket.com*; *Other:* Letter die cuts.

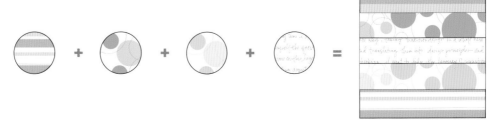

IT'S A PARTY BY ANNIE WEIS

why this works: Annie is so skilled at using **patterns** to help tell her stories. Strips of stripes, text and floral patterns combine with colorful photos and a big, happy title to document a birthday. Some stories simply beg for lots of color and pattern!

SUPPLIES *Textured cardstock:* Bazzill Basics Paper; *Patterned papers:* Imagination Project, Memories Complete and Scenic Route Paper Co.; *Letter stickers:* Gin-X, Imagination Project; *Ribbon:* Scrapworks; *Rubber stamps:* Fontwerks; *Stamping ink:* ColorBox, Clearsnap; *Canvas frame:* Li'l Davis Designs; *Leather flower, jelly stickers and decorative brad:* Making Memories; *Other:* Staples and brads.

 + + =

BE KIND BY ALI EDWARDS

why this works: Muted stripes create a **perfect home** for journaling. Take advantage of those straight lines to align photos, words and accents (such as the plastic letters here). When creating two-page spreads, I like to balance the entire layout by repeating each pattern on both sides. Sometimes they're in different proportions (such as a small strip on one page and a large block on the other), and in other instances they're equal.

SUPPLIES *Textured cardstock:* Bazzill Basics Paper and Die Cuts With a View; *Patterned papers:* foof-a-La (stripes), Autumn Leaves; KI Memories (floral); Wild Asparagus (circles), My Mind's Eye; *Trim:* Kollette, Colorbök; *Tag and tab:* SEI; *Plastic letters:* Autumn Leaves; *Rubber stamps:* PSX Design; *Stamping ink:* Ranger Industries; *Pen:* American Crafts.

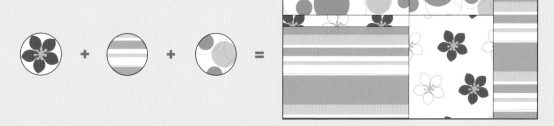

Learning and Dancing * AnCieNt MexiCAN Moving and Laughing * Trying and Loving * Singing and Joking * Talking and Making * Listening and Creating * Discovering

AfRo HaiTiaN dance Instrument Art * MartiAl ArTS * PeRcUssiON * FaBriC PriNtiNg * ART

arT & disCOVErY Camp

ART AND DISCOVERY CAMP BY ANNIE WEIS

why this works: On this layout, the patterned strips create a home for a very large rectangle gathering of photos. I love how Annie added one photo to each page that **breaks out of the structure** created by the strips, emphasizing the playful nature of the subject.

SUPPLIES *Textured cardstock:* Bazzill Basics Paper; *Patterned papers:* K&Company and Autumn Leaves; *Stickers:* Heidi Grace Designs, Doodlebug Design and Bo-Bunny Press; *Rub-ons:* Making Memories and Scrapworks; *Stamping Ink:* Adirondack, Ranger Industries.

SURPRISE VISIT BY ALI EDWARDS

why this works: I created patterned blocks to hold my journaling and additional title elements, then scattered these blocks over the two pages, varying their placement in between photos. You can design or embellish each of the blocks in the same way to add **consistency** within the overall design—try rounding corners, adding photo turns and tabs, using the same color and font, etc. Notice how the patterns on my layout don't really match any colors in the photos. I went more with the feel of the patterns (fun, light-hearted) to match the feelings I have about these memories.

SUPPLIES *Textured cardstock:* Bazzill Basics Paper; *Patterned papers:* Memory Box (stripes) and Making Memories (stripes and circles); *Rub-ons:* Li'l Davis Designs and 7gypsies; *Computer font:* 2Peas Stop Sign, downloaded from *www.twopeasinabucket.com*, Garamond, Microsoft Word; *Corner rounder:* EK Success; *Photo turns:* Making Memories.

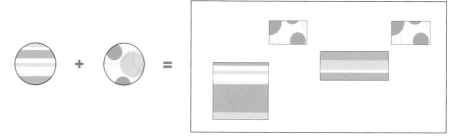

The journaling reads (handwritten): *This is YOUR thing. These trains. These little toys with funny faces and names and complete personalities. You love them. You wake-up thinking about them. Want to go right downstairs and check them out. "Merdock" is your current favorite. Followed closely by "Percy." You watch the videos. You make train noises. You drive them around and line them up... making sure they are in just the right spot.*

6 s 8 9 0 1 2 3 4 5 7

trains
YOUR THING

TRAINS BY ALI EDWARDS

why this works: Sometimes you want just a bit of pattern to liven up a layout. Why not lightly paint right on top of a busier pattern (such as the diagonal stripes here), let it dry, and then write or print your journaling directly on top of the painted area? Notice how the top stripe pattern is running vertically—it **balances** nicely with the visually strong horizontal patterned tape near the bottom of the layout.

SUPPLIES *Textured cardstock:* Bazzill Basics Paper; *Patterned paper and acrylic paint:* Making Memories; *Circle-number tape:* 7gypsies; *"S" accent:* Creative Imaginations; *Epoxy letters:* Karen Foster Design; *Label tape:* Dymo.

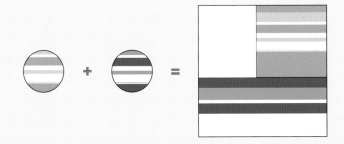

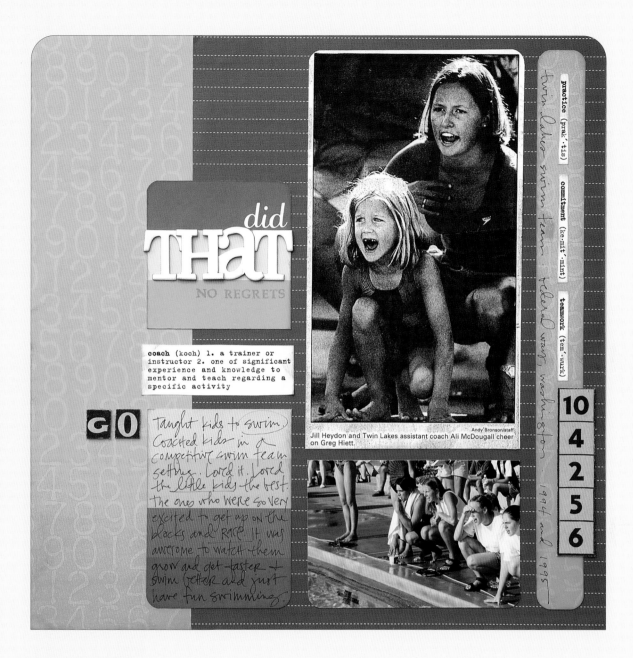

did
THaT
NO REGRETS

coach (koch) 1. a trainer or instructor 2. one of significant experience and knowledge to mentor and teach regarding a specific activity

GO Taught kids to swim. Coached kids in a competitive swim team setting. Loved it. Loved the little kids the best. The ones who were so very excited to get up on the blocks and race. It was awesome to watch them grow and get faster + swim better and just have fun swimming.

Jill Heydon and Twin Lakes assistant coach Ali McDougall cheer on Greg Hiett.

Andy Bronson/staff

practice (prak´tis)
commitment (ke·mit´ mint)
teamwork (tem´ wurk)

Twin Lakes swim team. Federal way, washington. 1994 and 1995

10
4
2
5
6

NO REGRETS BY ALI EDWARDS

why this works: This layout features three dominant vertical strips: the journaling/title block, the two photos set one on top of the other, and the patterned accent strip to the right of the photo. To even out the strong **vertical lines**, I used a brown stripe pattern as the largest part of the foundation. Finding that balance between vertical and horizontal elements helps create a well-designed page. Also, notice how the large striped patterned paper makes an excellent home for the title and journaling—don't be afraid to cut it up!

SUPPLIES *Textured cardstock:* Bazzill Basics Paper; *Patterned papers:* Chatterbox (stripes), SEI (stripes) and KI Memories (text); *Chipboard letters:* Heidi Swapp for Advantus; *Definition stickers:* Making Memories; *"No Regrets" rubber stamp:* River City Rubber Works; *Corner rounder:* Marvy Uchida; *Stamping ink:* ColorBox Fluid Chalk, Clearsnap.

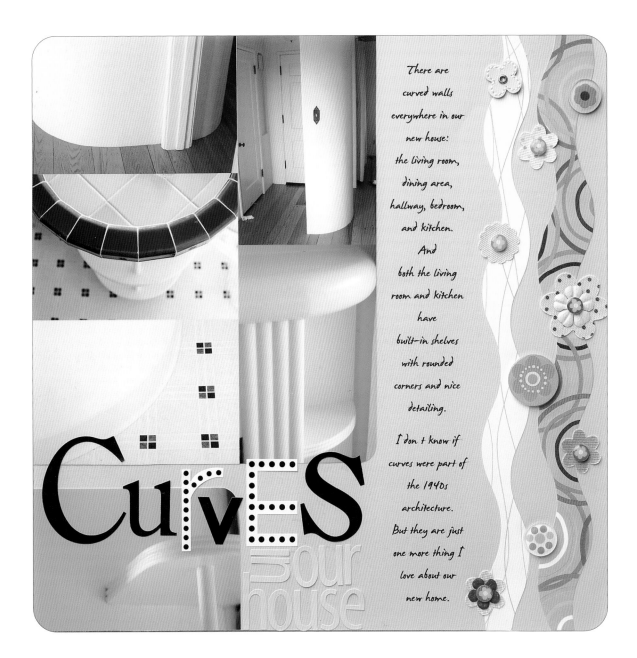

The journaling text on the layout reads:

There are curved walls everywhere in our new house: the living room, dining area, hallway, bedroom, and kitchen. And both the living room and kitchen have built-in shelves with rounded corners and nice detailing.

I don't know if curves were part of the 1940s architecture. But they are just one more thing I love about our new home.

CurvES =our house

CURVES BY ANNIE WEIS

why this works: A lovely random line pattern and a cropped circle pattern **blend** together well when they're cut with curved lines. The patterns echo the curves in the photos and provide a nice contrast to the photos' straight edges. The floral accents also help to soften and give additional visual weight to that area of the design.

SUPPLIES *Patterned papers:* KI Memories and Autumn Leaves; *Stickers:* Doodlebug Design; *Epoxy stickers:* Rob and Bob Studio, Provo Craft; *Canvas flowers:* foof-a-La, Autumn Leaves; *Paper flowers:* Prima; *Acrylic accents:* KI Memories; *Computer font:* James Faijardo, downloaded from the Internet.

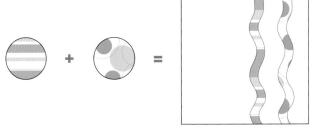

GOOD TIMES *in Cape Cod*

Colorful Creations **MEMORIES 2005**

staying at Tante's lovely home

1234567890
OOOOOO
lots of laughter

shopping around the Cape

Hope Live True
.Believe-Learn
Beauty Imagine
-Laugh.Cherish
Friends Family
.Journey.Dreams
Explore Inspire
-Love-Discover

having MOM be there with me

making many new friends in classes

it was absolutely fabulous

mom . me . Jenn . Jayne

TOday YOu with
Ali Edwards
OCtOber 23rd 2:30-3:30

colorful creations · cape cOd Ma

COLORFUL CREATIONS BY ALI EDWARDS

why this works: The large block of stamped squares **balances** the dominant vertical stripes on this layout. Vertical stripes often need to be balanced out in order for the layout to "feel" right. To help ground the page, I added the circle, clock and text stamps. I also used red rub-ons in the title to help balance the red stripes on the bottom.

SUPPLIES *Textured cardstock:* Bazzill Basics Paper; *Patterned papers:* Making Memories (cream) and 7gypsies (red); *Tab and rub-on stitching:* K&Company; *Rub-on letters:* Li'l Davis Designs and Making Memories; *Rubber stamps:* Technique Tuesday, 7gypsies and Stamp It!; *Pen:* American Crafts; *Stamping ink:* Versa Color, Tsukineko.

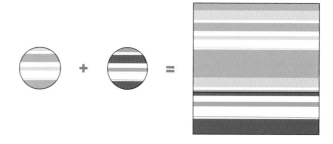

CAMPING PALS BY ALI EDWARDS

why this works: Another of my favorite ways to bring patterned papers together is to actually sew on the seams between the patterns. The quilt-like feeling adds a finished look to the edges of the patterns. After laying out the patterns and sewing the seams, I placed a gathering of photos on top and **linked** them all together by sanding around the outside edges. To solidify their relationship in a design sense, I added the "summer days" printed strip right over the middle of the photo seams.

SUPPLIES *Textured cardstock:* Bazzill Basics Paper and Die Cuts With a View; *Patterned papers:* Scenic Route Paper Co. (stripes), Pressed Petals (floral) and Cross-My-Heart (circles); *Chipboard letters and orange tape:* Heidi Swapp for Advantus; *Computer font:* AL Worn Machine, downloaded from *www.twopeasinabucket.com*; *Photo turns and index tab:* 7gypsies; *Brads:* Making Memories; *Rub-on stitched flowers:* Autumn Leaves; *Pen:* American Crafts.

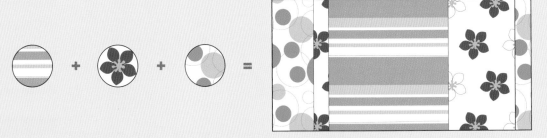

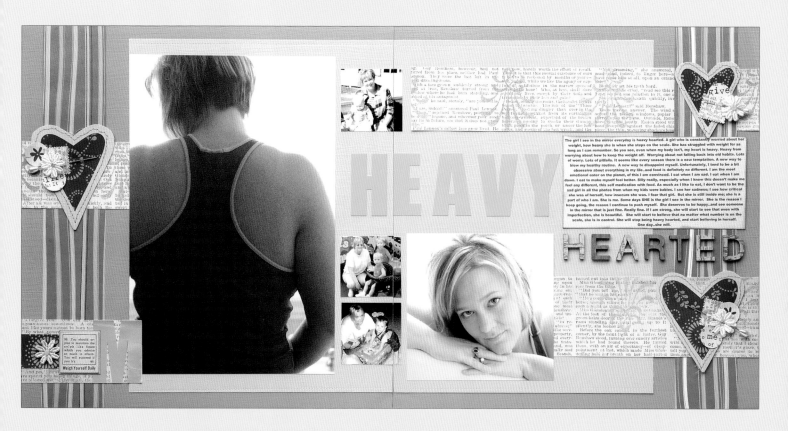

HEAVY HEARTED BY MILEY JOHNSON

why this works: Vertical strips of striped patterned paper create a beginning and an end (think book ends) and a home for accent **gatherings** on this well-designed layout. Miley also does a great job at creating accents made up of a variety of patterns. These accent gatherings support the theme and add visual interest to the layout.

SUPPLIES *Patterned papers:* KI Memories and Autumn Leaves; *Fortune:* Manto Fev; *Letter stickers:* SEI; *Wooden letters:* Li'l Davis Designs; *Pin and lace trim:* Making Memories.

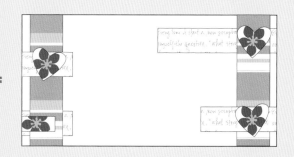

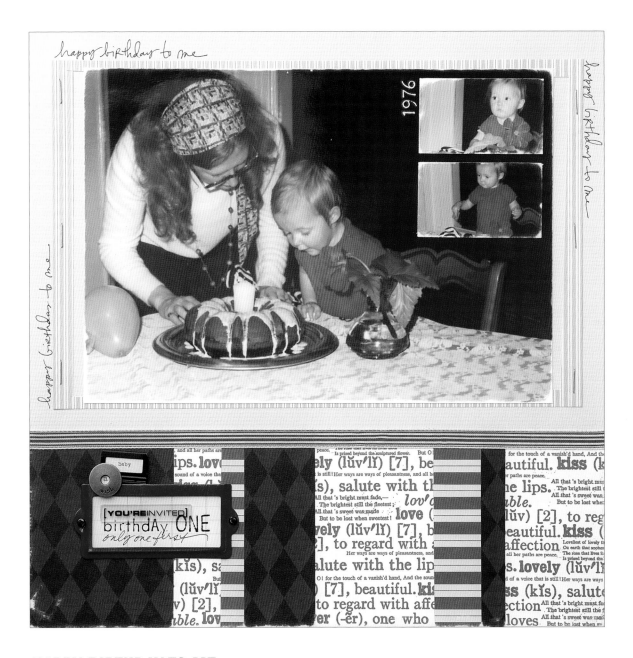

HAPPY BIRTHDAY TO ME BY ALI EDWARDS

why this works: The patterned block along the top of the layout creates one big strip upon which the focal-point photo sits. I cut a frame from a neutral striped pattern that **repeats** the lines in the patterned ribbon as well as the strong light-red striped pattern below. Notice how the reds in the bottom patterns don't match? Does it matter? Nope! You can successfully create a gathering of red patterns without finding that perfect match.

SUPPLIES *Textured cardstock:* Bazzill Basics Paper; *Patterned papers:* 7gypsies (text), Scenic Route Paper Co. (geometric), Mustard Moon (stripes) and Stampin' Up! (stripes); *Bookplate:* Art Warehouse, Creative Imaginations; *Rub-on letters:* Autumn Leaves; *Circle accent and epoxy phrase:* Making Memories; *Black tab:* 7gypsies; *Pen:* American Crafts.

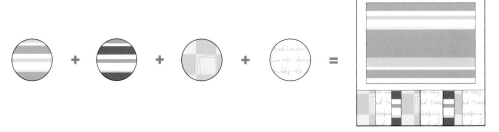

PLAY BY ALI EDWARDS

why this works: Do these patterns match this photo? A bit in their tone and color, but for the most part I chose these because I liked them. They made me happy. The photo makes me happy. Design-wise, the page works because I broke the patterns into sections (I used the back of a Heidi Swapp chipboard product package to create the sections) and chose patterns with various **densities** to complement the enlarged photo. The striped + text pattern is visually heavy because of the intricacy of its design (and how it fills up the paper with the pattern), the smaller floral pattern is lighter (showcasing more space between the elements within the pattern), and the whimsical line pattern is the lightest weight because it has the most white space between the lines.

SUPPLIES *Textured cardstock:* Bazzill Basics Paper; *Patterned papers:* foof-a-La (stripes) and MOD (floral), Autumn Leaves; KI Memories (stripes); *Letter stickers:* SEI; *Photo printing:* Scrapbookpictures.com; *Memo card:* 7gypsies; *Rub-on circle:* Memories Complete; *Chipboard packaging:* Heidi Swapp for Advantus.

I know all the words to the Spongebob theme song.
I have laugh lines around my eyes.
I have eaten more fruit snacks than any other adult I know.
I worry about the condition of our world.
I do more loads of laundry than I ever imagined I would do.
MY HEART IS FULL

REASONS BY MILEY JOHNSON

why this works: Three photos. Three patterns. Three tags. Three strips of patterned papers below and above the photos. All of these "threes" **combine** for a great design. Imagine this layout with the stripes oriented horizontally rather than vertically. The stripes' vertical orientation repeats the vertical nature of the photos (which is also repeated by the tags and the staples in the top-right corner), keeping the eye within the layout.

SUPPLIES *Patterned papers:* My Mind's Eye, KI Memories and Chatterbox; *Wooden letters:* Michaels; *Chipboard letters:* Li'l Davis Designs; *Tag:* Avery; *Computer font:* AL Outdoors, downloaded from *www.twopeasinabucket.com.*

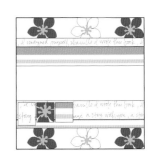

chapter summary

CHAPTER 3: STRIPES

1. *Rotate a horizontal print to a vertical orientation to get a whole new look on your page.*

2. *Direct the eye across your page with a strong directional stripe print.*

3. *Think of stripes as a tool you can use to align your photographs, words and accents.*

4. *Create your own striped background by cutting and combining a variety of patterned and journaling strips.*

5. *Soften a dominant stripe pattern by combining it with a soft floral print.*

6. *Mix and match horizontal and vertical prints on the same page.*

7. *Use a striped print as a baseline for handwriting your journaling.*

The best design does not come from knowing 3,000 typefaces and six Macintosh programs by heart. It comes from having a life and being observant and involved in the world at large.

Randall Balsmeyer

 text

PATTERNED PAPER

*I have to admit, I have a thing for text patterned papers.
You might have noticed I tend to use them quite a bit on my
scrapbook pages.*

That's because they're the ones in the store that catch my eye first. I'm drawn both to the prints that are legible and to the ones that are completely incomprehensible. I think part of it is because words are such a huge part of our lives. They have power in what we write and say—*and in what we don't.*

There's a comforting quality to text; when our eyes see a text pattern, it prepares our minds for learning, for listening, for absorbing information. Text can speak quietly or it can scream; it can reaffirm or surprise or even shock.

I think my passion for text began as a child. I loved books (still do). I loved seeing the combination of words and images in preschool board books. When I got older, I loved reading the words and then using my imagination to conjure up the images in my mind. And in high school, the walls of my room were covered with cool text and image combinations from magazines.

INSPIRATION BY ALI EDWARDS

SUPPLIES ON OPPOSITE PAGE *Textured cardstock:* Bazzill Basics Paper; *Patterned papers:* Danny O, K&Company; 7gypsies; *Patterned transparency:* 7gypsies; *Tag:* Narratives, Creative Imaginations; *Rub-ons:* Dee's Designs, My Mind's Eye; 7gypsies; KI Memories; *Rubber stamps:* Li'l Davis Designs; *Stamping ink:* ColorBox Fluid Chalk, Clearsnap.

Most of the time, when I'm working with text patterns, I'm using them more for the *design* of the print than for the words written on the paper. Text patterned paper conveys emotion, evokes memories and moves to its own unique beat depending on the typeface, color, size, sentiment, etc. Text can also help move your reader's eye across the layout in an expected pattern that has an orderly feel to it.

Text patterned paper is a natural for scrapbookers. Words tell a story; we "story-tell" on our layouts. By layering text paper onto our pages, we're helping to share the layers of a story. It's natural to combine text patterned paper with letter stickers and other alphabet-inspired embellishments (just think of the endless combinations you can create by combining text paper with rubber stamps, computer fonts, word squares, rub-ons, your own handwriting and more).

A text print is a patterned paper that includes words or images that mimic the look of printed and/or cursive handwriting. Text might represent the following ideas in art. Revise this list, add to it, make it your own.

- EDUCATION
- READING
- MESSAGE
- STORIES

- LEARNING
- COMMUNICATION
- LISTENING
- REFLECTIONS

- MEMORIES
- INFORMATION
- THOUGHTS
- FACTS

Choose text prints because you love them and because of the stories they can help you tell on your pages. In this chapter, I'll show you how.

silly girl

love (luv) n. ‖ <OE lufu ‖ 1 strong affection or liking for someone or something 2 a passionate aff
of one person for another 3 the object of such affection; a sweetheart 4 to feel love (for) - fall in love

1 2 3 4 5 6 7 8 9 0 1 2 3 4 5 6 7 8 9 0 1 2 3 4 5

jour·ney \júr-ní\ n 1 a travel or passage from one place to another   jour·ney \júr-ní\ n 1 a travel or passage from one

Yesterday will never return and tomorrow will
always be just out of reach. But today is always
present and it is this time when you are most
powerful and most in control to make things
happen. You make decisions right now. You act
right now. You live right now. | **Be proactive.**

SILLY GIRL BY ALI EDWARDS

why this works: Text goes with text. Just as circles are an easy complement to other circles, **text patterns tend to work well with other text patterns**. Cutting text patterns into strips and bringing in additional color accents to complete the overall look can result in a cool page that communicates a modern, fun feel. Overlap one strip over a vertical element (the journaling strip) to anchor it down on the page.

SUPPLIES *Textured cardstock:* Bazzill Basics Paper; *Patterned papers:* American Crafts, Arctic Frog, My Mind's Eye, Pebbles Inc. and 7gypsies; *Letter die cuts:* QuicKutz; *Ribbon:* 7gypsies; *Quote:* Stephen R. Covey.

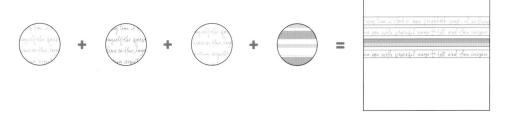

FAN BY MILEY JOHNSON

why this works: A red text background for a Big Red fan. Can't go wrong with that choice! I also love how Miley wasn't afraid to throw in another red-based text pattern for additional accents. It's all a part of the story she wants to tell.

SUPPLIES *Patterned papers:* Chatterbox, 7gypsies and Kangaroo and Joey; *Wooden letters:* Michaels; *Transparency:* Narratives, Creative Imaginations; *Rub-ons:* Chatterbox; *Tags:* Avery; *Letter stickers:* foof-a-La, Autumn Leaves; *Photo turns:* 7gypsies; *Brads:* Making Memories; *Eyelet brads:* Pebbles Inc.

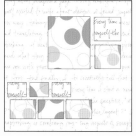

KAUAI 2005 BY ALI EDWARDS

why this works: I brought a bunch of patterns together by punching them into circles. Photo corners hold the gathering of photos and punched circles together. For this layout, I chose to go with warm-colored patterns (oranges and reds) as a nice complement to the warm tones in the photos.

SUPPLIES *Textured cardstock:* Bazzill Basics Paper; *Patterned papers:* 7gypsies (text), Chatterbox (red circles), My Mind's Eye (floral), KI Memories (floral) and Scrapworks (circles); *Canvas stickers and circle accent:* 7gypsies; *Rub-ons:* Making Memories; *Photo corners:* EK Success; *Circle punch:* Punch Bunch.

CAPTURING ... BY JAMIE WATERS. PHOTO BY TARA WHITNEY.

why this works: Would this layout work without the patterned strips along the bottom? Yep. Does it work with the patterns? Yep. Patterns are as much about **personal expression** as they are about serious design function. Here, the little strips, especially the torn text strip, say just a bit more about the Waters family.

SUPPLIES *Patterned papers:* 7gypsies and K&Company; *Acrylic "W":* KI Memories; *Bottle cap:* Li'l Davis Designs; *Index tab:* 7gypsies; *Label tape:* Dymo.

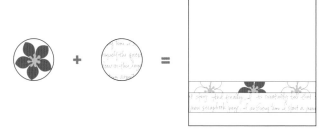

It can be hazy, cloudy, foggy, sunny, or smoggy. We just can't get enough of the view from our living room. Most days, there's a haze hanging over the City. Or there's so much fog we can't make out any of the bridges or even the downtown Oakland skyline.

But then there are days when the air is crisp and clean. You can see every detail for miles and miles. Mount Tamalpais, the Golden Gate, Telegraph Hill, the Transamerica building, the Bay Bridge, Treasure Island, Twin Peaks... we can see it all. And it feels like we're on top of the world.

VIEW OF THE CITY BY ANNIE WEIS

why this works: Make it easy on yourself and choose text patterns that already communicate part of the message you want to convey. Annie chose this text pattern from 7gypsies that features the words "Most Memorable." To complete the thought, she stamped "October" directly onto the patterned paper for a cool secondary title. Also, notice how Annie placed the darker, denser text pattern along the bottom, anchoring and balancing the layout.

SUPPLIES *Patterned papers:* Scenic Route Paper Co. and 7gypsies; *Transparency:* OfficeMax; *Stickers:* American Crafts, Memories Complete and 7gypsies; *Rub-ons and brad:* Making Memories; *Ribbon:* Scrapworks; *Rubber stamps:* Educational Insights, Inc.; *Stamping Ink:* ColorBox, Clearsnap; *Metal letters and pen:* American Crafts; *Computer font:* Blue Highway, downloaded from the Internet; *Other:* Staples.

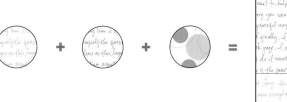

WORK BASKETS 2005 BY ALI EDWARDS

why this works: Many times **my photos are just about enough** to communicate the story I want to tell. To add a bit of pattern to this layout, I included a strip of text-patterned tape and a thin strip of striped ribbon. The text-patterned tape evokes thoughts of the happiness and love that comes through learning. I added a small bit of handwritten journaling directly to the photos for additional details.

SUPPLIES *Textured cardstock:* Bazzill Basics Paper; *Patterned tape:* 7gypsies; *Ribbon:* Maya Road; *Rub-on letters:* Scrapworks; *Pen:* American Crafts; *Rubber stamps:* Technique Tuesday; *Stamping ink:* StazOn, Tsukineko.

 =

AND SO IT ALL BEGAN BY ANNIE WEIS

why this works: Love is vibrant. Vibrant love begs for vibrant patterns, including text that shouts instead of whispers. Notice how the first text pattern on the left is the loudest of the three text patterns? It moves down in volume as you approach the cardstock at the other end. Annie brought all of this together with red and green accents that work well with the colors in the patterns.

SUPPLIES *Textured cardstock:* Bazzill Basics Paper; *Patterned papers:* Autumn Leaves, Scenic Route Paper Co. and 7gypsies; *Rub-ons:* KI Memories and Scrapworks; *Ribbon:* May Arts, Doodlebug Design and Making Memories; *Metal letters:* American Crafts; *Fabric:* Amy Butler; *Vellum quotations:* Autumn Leaves; *Computer font:* Day of the Tentacle, downloaded from the Internet; *Other:* Staples.

LOVE YOU, SIMON BY ALI EDWARDS

why this works: I combined patterns effectively on my layout by cutting them into equal-sized shapes and using each square as a home for an accent. I scattered my photos between the square shapes. To show how they all work together as one large element, I rounded the corners of the outer four squares and rectangles.

SUPPLIES *Textured cardstock:* Bazzill Basics Paper; *Patterned papers:* Scenic Route Paper Co. (text), My Mind's Eye (floral) and Paper Source (art); *Quote accents:* My Mind's Eye; *Square accents:* KI Memories and Heidi Swapp for Advantus; *Green tag:* Li'l Davis Designs; *Chipboard letters:* Li'l Davis Designs and Heidi Swapp for Advantus; *Ribbon:* Scrapworks; *Silver accent:* Pebbles Inc.; *Rubber stamps:* Turtle Press; *Letter stickers and pen:* American Crafts.

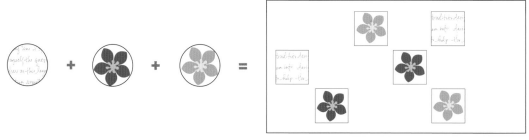

TOTAL ENTERTAINMENT BY JAMIE WATERS

why this works: Colorful life photos call for equally colorful patterns. Here, Jamie brought four patterns together, linking them through their colors, and added accents and rub-ons that reemphasize the color choices. Using patterned papers as frames is a great way to begin adding patterns to your layouts.

SUPPLIES *Patterned papers:* KI Memories, Doodlebug Design and Autumn Leaves; *Acrylic shapes, rub-on letters and quote sticker:* KI Memories; *Rub-on flowers:* Scrapworks; *Pen:* American Crafts.

 + + + =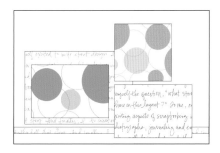

HALLOWEEN BY ALI EDWARDS

why this works: Themed text paper is a natural choice for telling stories. Rather than using an entire sheet, try cutting it up and creating blocks that serve as homes for photos, journaling, etc. Also, be on the lookout for titles that can be pulled directly from text patterned paper (such as the "Halloween" title featured here).

SUPPLIES *Textured cardstock:* Bazzill Basics Paper; *Patterned papers:* KI Memories (orange text) and Rusty Pickle (Halloween text); *Rub-ons:* Fontwerks (dots and flowers) and Li'l Davis Designs (numbers); *Computer font:* Verdana, Microsoft Word.

 + =

MIRROR IMAGE BY MILEY JOHNSON

why this works: **Cut up those text patterns** into rectangles for a whole new combination of patterns.
Break up the hard lines of the text-patterned strips with circles cut from patterned paper and flower accents.
Great balance here between photo, pattern and journaling.

SUPPLIES *Patterned papers:* 7gypsies and All My Memories; *Jump rings:* Junkitz; *Flowers:* Michaels; *Rub-ons:* Jeneva & Company; *Word phrases:* 7gypsies; *Computer font:* Unknown.

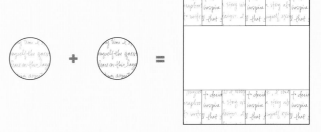

designer insight

I asked the contributors to my book for their best tips for choosing and using patterned paper on their layouts. Here's what Miley shared with me:

MILEY JOHNSON

1. *Choose colors and patterns that visually connect.* I like to start by looking at the colors in my photographs and then choosing patterned paper that reflects that color scheme. When I choose two or more patterns that work together, I like for them to visually connect. For example, your eye can easily "see" two different square patterns. I've also found that there are certain neutral colors that almost always work together.

2. *Repeat bits and pieces of patterned paper as part of your overall page design.* I like using squares or circles of patterned paper as embellishments for the centers of flowers or to fill in random squares in a pattern. Think of using bits and pieces of patterned paper anywhere you'd use a traditional embellishment (such as a brad or a button).

3. *Create a custom page background by mixing and matching favorite strips of patterned paper.* I unify the patterns on my page by stitching them together or by lining them up square with each other.

4. *Think of your page's message and choose papers accordingly.* I've found that patterned papers are a powerful way to communicate a wide range of emotions, from soft and sleepy to bold and energetic.

SWEET DREAMS BY MILEY JOHNSON

why this works: I love how the large circle envelopes the focal-point photo. The text pattern within the circle evokes a sense of nostalgia. The contrast between the bright floral patterns and the soft text pattern is perfectly in line with what Miley wanted to communicate on her layout: the give and take of childhood and growing up.

SUPPLIES *Patterned papers:* 7gypsies; Michael Miller; KI Memories; foof-a-La, Autumn Leaves; *Plastic letters:* Heidi Swapp for Advantus; *Leather flowers:* Urban Art; *Rhinestone brads:* SEI; *Letter stickers:* KI Memories; *Paper flowers:* Prima; *Computer font:* 2Peas Red Velvet Cake, downloaded from *www.twopeasinabucket.com*.

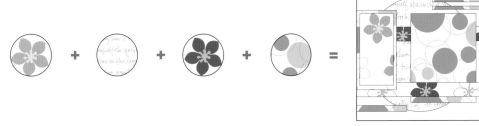

LOVE YOU, DADDY BY ALI EDWARDS

why this works: A nice streamlined patterned paper combination in the backgroud lays the foundation for an off-center, angled photo placement. Use words and letters within the patterned paper (like the "u" here) to help tell your story. Notice how the punch was used on the photos and the patterned paper is peeking through - photos are fair game for being punched too!

SUPPLIES *Cardstock:* Bazzill; *Patterned Paper:* GinX, Anna Griffin; *Cardstock Strip:* Making Memories; *Circle Stamp:* Savvy Stamps; *Ink:* Versa Color; *Punch:* Punch Bunch; *Stick Pins:* Making Memories.

 + **=**

(gOd bleSs)

eVeNiNiNg PRAYER *each and every night*

Dear Lord I thank You for Your care.

You've been right with me everywhere.

At school, at play, You're by my side.

My special Friend, my loving Guide.

And when the sun has said goodbye,

and little stars shine in the sky,

You're still with me, not far above.

You're in my heart for You are love.

the same one I said as a child

EVENING PRAYER BY ALI EDWARDS

why this works: Sometimes it's easier to work with text patterns if you can **imagine the words simply as lines rather than words to read**. Three patterns are showcased here—each features soft text. The three vertical rectangles mimic the vertical stripes in the couch (lower photo) and serve as a nice contrast to the typed, horizontal journaling strips. The torn edges of the patterns along the top soften the overall look and feel of the page. Also, notice how I included a small amount of the large pattern from the right side on the top of the left side—as I was working, I felt I needed to show some of that pattern on the left side of the photo to achieve an overall sense of balance.

SUPPLIES *Textured cardstock:* Bazzill Basics Paper; *Patterned papers:* 7gypsies, Autumn Leaves and Making Memories; *Rubber stamps:* PSX Design; *"S":* Heidi Swapp for Advantus; *Stamping ink:* VersaColor, Tsukineko; *Computer font:* Avant Garde, downloaded from the Internet; *Pen:* American Crafts.

Scrapbook Layout

Name _Cameron waters_   Date _9-14-2005_

1. In school, the thing I like to do best is _arts and crafts_

2. Outside of school, the thing I like to do best is _play hand ball_

3. When I grow up I will _make a movi_

4. I don't like _sepl playing tag_
5. My favorite animal is _turtle_
6. The best sport is _fot ball_
7. The person I like best is _family_
8. When nobody is around I like to _draw_

9. Next summer I hope to _go to Arsvellea_

10. My favorite place to be is _home_
11. What I think is funny is _cata geting shaved_

age 6. 2nd grade.

he said

things i like

A B C D E F G H I J K L M N O P Q R S T U V W

THINGS I LIKE BY JAMIE WATERS

why this works: **Everyday papers** that tell the stories of our lives are always a welcome addition to a layout—especially when they include children's handwriting. The less-readable text pattern (above the photo) contrasts wonderfully with the very legible alphabet strip along the bottom. Notice how the buttons down the right side seem to perfectly finish off the page? The repetition of colors from the dominant pattern on the left brings balance and a feeling of completion to the layout.

SUPPLIES *Patterned papers:* Li'l Davis Designs, Autumn Leaves and BasicGrey; *Letter stickers:* Doodlebug Design; *Tab and fabric word:* 7gypsies; *Buttons:* SEI.

 + =

LOVE, RUN AND PLAY BY ALI EDWARDS

why this works: Text papers with **legible words** are a great option for enhancing a layout. Here, I combined three sheets of the same text pattern in three different colors for added interest and variety. The handwriting mixed with printed text plays into the overall sense of play, fun and the goodness of life. The design is fairly simple: a background foundation with four patterns on each page (mirror image from one side to the other) + white cardstock and photos on top. I could have chosen any number of patterned papers for a layout about the beach; these are the ones that spoke loudest to me.

SUPPLIES *Textured cardstock:* Bazzill Basics Paper; *Patterned papers:* 7gypsies (text) and Scrapworks (floral); *Stickers:* Scrapworks; *Rub-on:* 7gypsies.

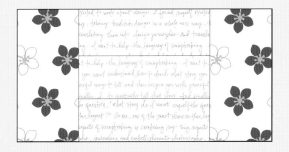

One of our very favorite ways to see the sights. By boat.

SUMMER 2005
SYDNEY, AUSTRALIA

SYDNEY HARBOUR BY JAMIE WATERS

why this works: The text pattern here creates a sense of adventure, of history, of travel. I also appreciate how the tiny strip of circle-patterned vellum along the bottom repeats the circles in the journaling tags.

SUPPLIES *Patterned papers:* SEI and Autumn Leaves; *Letter stickers:* Wordsworth; *Pocket:* Li'l Davis Designs; *Ribbon:* Strano; *Metal plaque:* K&Company; *Computer font:* AL Remington, downloaded from *www.twopeasinabucket.com.*

 + =

KAUAI GIRLS BY ALI EDWARDS

why this works: Viewing patterns is a lot about perception. Striped patterns can look like geometric patterns. Stripes can come together to create diamonds. Does any of it matter? Nope. It's really more about going with the flow. Choosing what speaks to you in the moment. Playing and having fun. One of the things that makes this page works is the repetition of horizontal lines: the ribbon, the filmstrip, the strip of green patterned paper, the horizontal line created by the rub-ons and letter stickers between the two photos.

SUPPLIES *Textured cardstock:* Bazzill Basics Paper; *Patterned papers:* Nostalgiques (text), EK Success; Polar Bear Press (geometric); Paperfever (stripes); *Rub-ons:* Jeneva & Company, 7gypsies and KI Memories; *Letter stickers:* American Crafts; *Pens:* Creative Memories; Zig Millennium, EK Success; *Corner rounder:* Marvy Uchida; *Rubber stamps:* PSX Design; *Stamping ink:* Stampin' Up!; *Ribbon:* May Arts; *Filmstrip:* Junkyard Art; *Paper clip:* K&Company.

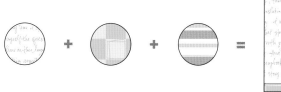

MAY YOU ALWAYS LEARN BY ALI EDWARDS

why this works: For this layout, I chose three patterns that demonstrate an **equal visual weight**—no one pattern really stands out on this spread. I wanted the text pattern to repeat the theme of learning. Notice how these three patterns don't fight for your attention. They **blend** into the background, giving center stage to the photos and journaling.

SUPPLIES *Textured cardstock:* Bazzill Basics Paper; *Patterned papers:* Wild Asparagus (circles), My Mind's Eye; KI Memories (text); Memories Complete (stitched line); *Computer font:* Garamond, Microsoft Word; *Rub-on:* Die Cuts With a View; *Rubber stamps:* Making Memories; *Stamping ink:* ColorBox Fluid Chalk, Clearsnap.

 + + =

AMAZING EYE BY JAMIE WATERS

why this works: **Beauty in simplicity and restraint**. Here, Jamie neatly tucked five little strips of patterned papers between the large leaf photo and the photo of her son, and layered a piece of a text-printed transparency over them to link the patterns together visually. I love how Jamie made the patterns a seamless element.

SUPPLIES *Patterned papers:* Autumn Leaves; *Transparency:* Narratives, Creative Imaginations; *Rub-ons and epoxy letter:* Li'l Davis Designs; *Photo turn:* 7gypsies; *Photo corners:* Chatterbox; *Pen:* American Crafts.

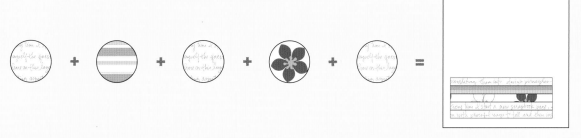

FOR ME BY JAMIE WATERS

why this works: Jamie added text patterns to this page without worrying about the direction the text was going. You can use text patterns both horizontally and vertically. **Don't get hung up on the idea that you need to be able to read the writing.** Instead, look to qualities such as size, scale, shape, mood and color; choose text patterns that will complement the story you want to communicate.

SUPPLIES *Patterned papers, letter swirl and sticker tab:* 7gypsies; *Rub-on letters:* BasicGrey; *Pen:* American Crafts.

SPECIAL DAYS BY ALI EDWARDS

why this works: Busy patterns often call for a crisp white mat to bring the photos and journaling forward within your design. Layer a couple of text patterns on top of each other and tear the top one to reveal the bottom pattern—this is a great way to add a bit of bold color to an overall beige text pattern. Utilize the lines on a striped pattern as a home for journaling.

SUPPLIES *Textured cardstock:* Bazzill Basics Paper; *Patterned papers:* Marah Johnson (text), Creative Imaginations; Danny O (text), K&Company; Magic Scraps (stripes); *Fabric tags:* Scrapworks; *Stickers:* 7gypsies; *Rubber stamps:* Provo Craft; *Stamping ink:* ColorBox Fluid Chalk, Clearsnap; *Pen:* Zig Millennium, EK Success; *Other:* Staples.

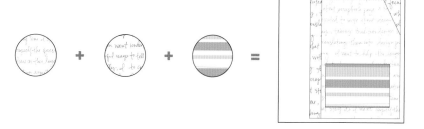

SCHOOL DAYS BY ANNIE WEIS

why this works: This layout showcases a nice gathering of rectangle-based patterned-paper shapes, complemented by rectangle frames in the lower-right corner. Cool vintage text patterns and handwritten journaling from Annie's daughter complete the look.

SUPPLIES *Textured cardstock:* Bazzill Basics Paper; *Patterned papers:* Imagination Project, Li'l Davis Designs and Scenic Route Paper Co.; *Stickers:* me & my BIG ideas and Memories Complete; *Rub-ons:* Autumn Leaves; *Ribbon:* May Arts; *Tags and leather frames:* Li'l Davis Designs; *Acetate accents:* KI Memories.

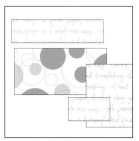

chapter summary

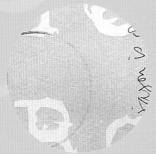

1. *Select bold text patterns to shout a message on your page.*

2. *Choose text patterns that already communicate part of the message you want to convey.*

3. *Break up the hard lines of text-patterned strips with circles cut from patterned paper and flower accents.*

4. *Imagine the words on text patterns simply as lines rather than words to read.*

5. *Combine sheets of the same text pattern in different colors to create a unified look on your page.*

6. *Position text patterns either horizontally or vertically.*

7. *Apply the same design rules to a text pattern as you would a striped pattern.*

Everything I touch, see, smell, hear and experience is subject
to use in my work. the same is true for everyone I
encounter. I believe this to be true for everyone,
whether we are conscious of it or not.

Sharoz Makarechi

geometric
PATTERNED PAPER

Ah, geometry. Remember those good old days?

Geometry was one of my toughest subjects in high school. All those
lines and points and angles and figures—who knew there were so many
different kinds of shapes? Hand me a thick literature or history book
and I was all over it. *But geometry?* It just didn't speak to me. And to
be honest, I didn't care about it all that much. I'm not sure how many
times I complained, "I will never use this."

Of course, I made it through geometry and went on to graduate.
Looking back now, *with a bit of perspective*, I do remember fondly
doodling squares and rectangles and diamonds and triangles all over
my brown grocery bag–covered textbook. Even back then there was
something about shapes that was attractive to me. (But not enough to
make me love geometry.)

Today, as a designer, I work with basic geometric shapes all the time. I
rely on them to add structure to my layouts. To create order. To give
homes to accents, embellishments and journaling. To establish consistency within my designs.

CRAZY TRAVEL BY ALI EDWARDS

SUPPLIES ON OPPOSITE PAGE *Textured cardstock:* Bazzill Basics Paper; *Patterned papers:* 7gypsies and K&Company; *Small note cards:* Lotta Jansdotter; *Rubber stamps:* Fontwerks (large parentheses), Cavallini & Co. (letters) and Making Memories (months); *Rub-ons:* Dee's Designs, My Mind's Eye; *Stamping ink:* Stampin' Up!; *Pen:* American Crafts; *Tags:* 7gypsies; *Word sticker:* K&Company.

One of my favorite ways to incorporate geometric shapes into my layouts is with punches. *I am in love with my square punch.* It could be my all-time favorite tool. Punched patterned-paper squares are something I doubt I will ever tire of using on my pages. And once you find something you love, there's nothing wrong with using it over and over again!

So let's take a look at creating and playing with geometric patterns. And no tests, I promise!

A geometric print is a patterned paper that predominantly features squares, rectangles, diamonds or other geometric shapes (with the exception of *circles*, which are so cool they get their own category— see Chapter 1).

Geometric shapes often represent the following ideas in art. Revise this list, add to it, make it your own.

- DEFINITION
- SERIOUS
- ARTISTIC
- MOTION

- REPETITION
- SYMBOLIC
- CLASSIC
- ORDER
- UNITY

- ELEGANT
- STRENGTH
- CONTEMPORARY VALUES

Choose geometric prints because you love them and because of the stories they can help you tell on your pages. In this chapter, I'll show you how.

HE'S LIKE THAT BY MILEY JOHNSON

why this works: Geometric shapes, especially diamonds, are great for establishing **direction**. The diamond strips along the top and bottom borders point into the middle of the layout, keeping your eye on the focal-point photo. The title grabs your attention with the "H" accent piece, then directs your eye down to the bottom photo and the journaling. The horizontal diamond pattern aligns perfectly with the journaling and moves you into the bottom row of large diamonds, bringing you back to the focal-point photo.

SUPPLIES *Patterned papers:* BasicGrey, Autumn Leaves, Making Memories and Chatterbox; *Letter stickers:* SEI; *Chipboard letter:* Chatterbox; *Ribbon:* May Arts; *Metal frame:* Making Memories; *Buttons:* Junkitz; *Chipboard strips:* Heidi Swapp for Advantus; *Computer fonts:* AL Patriot, downloaded from www.twopeasinabucket.com; Arial, Microsoft Word.

DETERMINATION

Love seeing you get out there and get in the action. You always seem pleasantly surprised to see how much fun you end up having.

STRENGTH

GO 4 IT BY JAMIE WATERS

why this works: Jamie created four blocks of content: two photos, a title block and a journaling block. How does she make it all work? She **repeated** elements diagonally: two raised, white rectangle word accents and the blue color. Just that little bit of added blue within the title brings the entire layout together. I also love the little collage of tags under the journaling.

SUPPLIES *Patterned papers:* Scrapworks; *Tag die cuts:* KI Memories; *Ribbon strip, epoxy letter, ribbon slider and clay phrases:* Li'l Davis Designs; *Letter stickers:* Gin-X, Imagination Project; *Pen:* American Crafts.

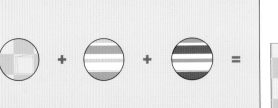
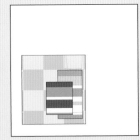

REALLY BY JAMIE WATERS

why this works: It's all about those strips. A great gathering of patterns that evoke goodness, gladness and happiness. Light, bright patterns—each with a bit of green and/or light brown (repeated in the title section)—**unify** the page.

SUPPLIES *Patterned papers:* Li'l Davis Designs, SEI, K&Company, KI Memories and Scrapworks; *Ribbon and stickers:* Li'l Davis Designs; *Fabric word:* 7gypsies; *Letter stamps:* Li'l Davis Designs ("Really") and Educational Insights; *Pen:* American Crafts.

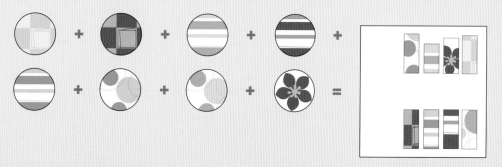

SCHOOL ART BY JAMIE WATERS

why this works: Geometric patterns tend to work well when they're cut down into smaller sections. For this layout, Jamie chose patterns that echo many of the colors in her photos and evoke a light, whimsical, artistic feel. One of my favorite elements on this page is in the title—the word "School" includes the interior of two different-colored "o" stickers. A totally clever way to use those leftover items!

SUPPLIES *Patterned papers:* KI Memories and American Crafts; *Acrylic letters and circle die cut:* KI Memories; *Letter and tab stickers:* Doodlebug Design; *Concho:* Scrapworks.

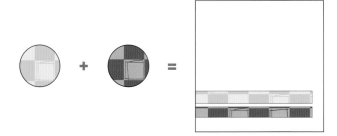

SING, SING BY ANNIE WEIS

why this works: Annie brought a variety of patterns together by working with them as if they were pieces of a quilt. It's easy to do: Punch an array of patterned papers into squares. Sew stitches or use rub-on stitches at a diagonal to create the look of real quilting. Add elements directly to the squares—consider letter stickers, rub-ons, circle accents and more. Here, Annie **unified the patterns** through shape (the squares) and through color (most of the patterns feature a warm yellowish-orange).

SUPPLIES *Patterned papers:* American Crafts, BasicGrey, Chatterbox, Daisy D's Paper Co., Design Originals, Doodlebug Design, Fiber Scraps, KI Memories, Li'l Davis Designs, Scrapworks and 7gyspies; *Stickers:* Provo Craft; *Rub-ons:* Doodlebug Design, Heidi Swapp for Advantus and Autumn Leaves; *Ribbon:* Scenic Route Paper Co. and Doodlebug Design; *Rubber stamps:* Fontwerks and Impress Rubber Stamps; *Stamping ink:* VersaColor, Tsukineko; *Tag:* Li'l Davis Designs; *Mini file folder:* Creative Imaginations; *Brad:* Making Memories; *Pen:* Zig Writer, EK Success; *Square punch:* Creative Memories; *Concho:* Scrapworks.

OUR HOME BY VANESSA REYES

why this works: Geometric patterns create a great **foundation** upon which to build the rest of your layout. Crop photos into rectangles and squares, and place them inside one large square of patterned paper. I also love how Vanessa added three additional accents: the large circle and the two rectangles with rounded corners.

SUPPLIES *Patterned papers:* Chatterbox and American Crafts; *Die cuts, photo corners, chipboard corners and flower:* Chatterbox; *Heart, crystal brads and plaques:* Making Memories; *Plastic letter:* Heidi Swapp for Advantus.

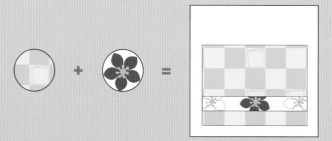

WIPE OUT BY VANESSA REYES

why this works: I love this layout. I feel like I'm there, experiencing the craziness of a wipe-out. The mishmash of elements in the title section, the photos placed at angles, the "X" created with ribbon—all of these things work together to communicate the essence of the story. Vanessa brought out the red color from both geometric patterns as a good jumping-off point for the rest of her accents. Great **color** choice.

SUPPLIES *Patterned papers, chipboard corners and photo corners:* Chatterbox; *Chipboard letters:* Heidi Swapp for Advantus; *Metal letters, tags, staples and ribbon:* Making Memories; *Bookplate and label sticker:* Li'l Davis Designs.

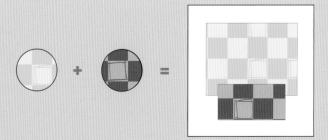

DIRTY SOCKS BY MILEY JOHNSON

why this works: Everyday life. The stuff that matters. The enlarged photo of Miley's son's socks is wonderfully paired with masculine brown-tone geometric patterns. Feel free to print your journaling right on your patterned paper; on this layout, it's the perfect location. Red **accents** worked in here and there complete the look.

SUPPLIES *Patterned papers:* Chatterbox and Junkitz; *Chipboard letters and heart:* Making Memories; *Metal clip, photo turns and canvas hanger:* Junkitz; *Phrase die cut:* Chatterbox; *Computer font:* Unknown.

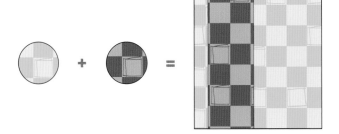

CELEBRATE BY JAMIE WATERS

why this works: One of the things I love most about this page is that Jamie used muted tones to express a feeling of celebration. When I think of the word "celebrate," I usually think of light, bright colors. The **tones** Jamie chose, however, come directly from her photo. She not only brought out the browns, but also the blues and sage greens as well. It all works together so nicely. It feels complete.

SUPPLIES *Patterned papers:* Li'l Davis Designs and KI Memories; *Letter stickers:* American Crafts.

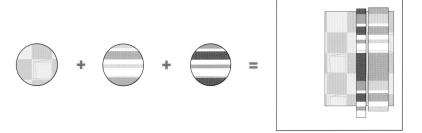

designer insight

I asked the contributors to my book for their best tips for choosing and using patterned paper on their layouts. Here are my answers to the same question:

ALI EDWARDS

1. *Cut it. Tear it. Punch it.* Patterned paper was designed to be played with and manipulated! I almost never use a full sheet of patterned paper on a single-page layout. You'll notice that strips are huge for me. I love being able to trim or rip paper into strips and use them on a page.

2. *Start with cardstock.* Yep, this is a book on patterned paper, but I always use cardstock as the starting place for my page. It's the base of my page. It's my blank canvas. When I start with a neutral background, I can easily add bits and pieces of color as needed without my layout looking too busy.

3. *Start with your photos.* It's an old-school approach, but I believe in looking to my photographs for color and design inspiration. Using patterned paper on your layouts can really be as simple as looking at your photographs, choosing a color, and then going through your patterned paper collections and finding patterns that complement that color.

4. *Experiment.* Mix and match manufacturers. Let go of the feeling that things need to match exactly or that all of your papers need to come from the same manufacturer. In fact, many of my patterned-paper combinations have been a result of trial and error (also known as play).

PROM MEMORIES BY MILEY JOHNSON

why this works: Geometric, black-and-white patterns have a formal, modern feel—a great choice for a layout about prom. Pair those with a neutral text print for a great combination that lets the photos stand out. Miley took **colors** directly from her photos to use as accents, including an additional patterned paper with pink diamonds.

SUPPLIES *Patterned papers:* KI Memories, 7gypsies and Anna Griffin; *Wooden letters and stencil stickers:* Li'l Davis Designs; *Paper flowers:* Prima; *Rhinestone pin:* EK Success; *"Memories" epoxy accent and buttons:* Junkitz; *Tag:* Avery; *Other:* Ribbon.

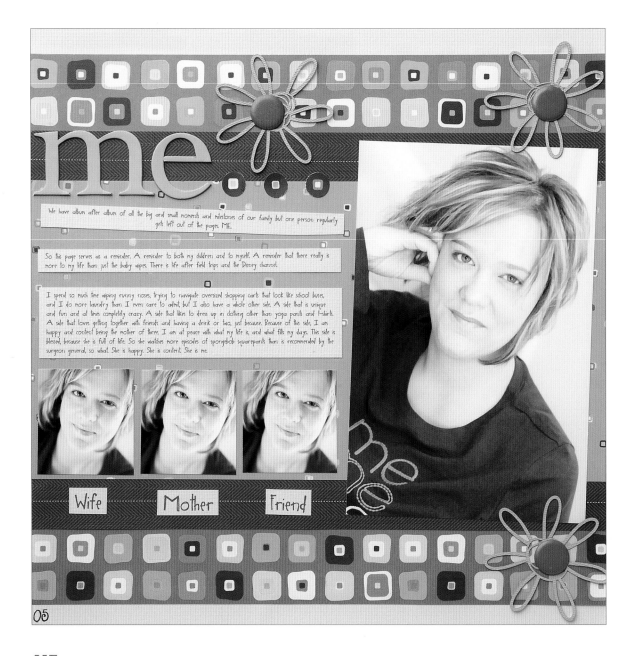

We have album after album of all the big and small moments and milestones of our family but one person regularly gets left out of the pages: ME.

So this page serves as a reminder. A reminder to both my children and to myself. A reminder that there really is more to my life than just the baby wipes. There is life after field trips and the Disney channel.

I spend so much time wiping runny noses, trying to navigate oversized shopping carts that look like school buses, and I do more laundry than I even care to admit, but I also have a whole other side. A side that is unique and fun and at times completely crazy. A side that likes to dress up in clothing other than yoga pants and t-shirts. A side that loves getting together with friends and having a drink or two, just because. Because of this side, I am happy and content being the mother of three. I am at peace with what my life is, and what fills my days. This side is blessed, because she is full of life. So she watches more episodes of spongebob squarepants than is recommended by the surgeon general, so what. She is happy. She is content. She is me.

Wife   Mother   Friend

05

ME BY MILEY JOHNSON

why this works: Another way to create **harmony** among patterned papers is to use the same basic geometric pattern in different sizes (such as large squares with small squares, as seen here on Miley's layout). The larger, square patterned-paper strips frame the content while the smaller, more open-square patterned paper becomes home to journaling strips and supporting photos. Three large flower die cuts form a lovely visual triangle around the focal-point photo.

SUPPLIES *Patterned papers:* KI Memories and Chatterbox; *Chipboard letters:* Heidi Swapp for Advantus; *Flower die cuts:* Deluxe Designs; *Brads:* Bazzill Basics Paper; *Computer font:* 2Peas Red Velvet, downloaded from *www.twopeasinabucket.com.*

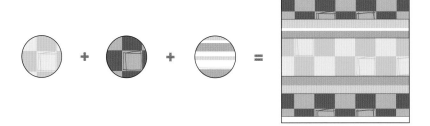

The best foliage always takes me by surprise.

It could be a tiny Japanese maple or a row of Liquid Amber trees in Piedmont.

Or this Scarlet Oak in Redwood Heights.

TurNing Leaves

Maybe we can't match New England,

but we do have beautiful fall colors.

And our trees have the coolest names...

1. Liquid Amber/
2. Gum tree
3. Scarlet Oak
4. Ginkgo
5. Chinese Pistache
6. California Pepper
7. Sugar Maple
8. Tulip tree
9. Grape Myrtle
10. Redbud

TURNING LEAVES BY ANNIE WEIS

why this works: On this layout, Annie literally **repeated** the leaves from her photo and added additional flower accents cut from a variety of patterned papers. Notice how, in this case, the patterns take a backseat to the colors within the patterns. In general, the smaller you cut a pattern, the more it becomes about the color. Annie also reminds us that geometric patterns don't have to be cut into geometric shapes.

SUPPLIES *Patterned papers:* KI Memories, Heidi Grace Designs and Scrapworks; *Journaling tags:* 7gypsies; *Stickers:* Close To My Heart and Sandylion; *Letter stickers:* Autumn Leaves; *Tab:* Scrapworks; *Computer font:* American Type Condensed, downloaded from the Internet; *Pen:* EK Success.

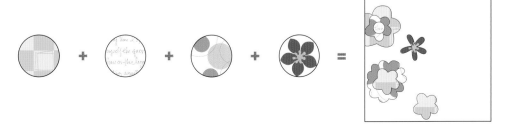

FAIRY FRIENDS BY ANNIE WEIS

why this works: Don't forget about cool geometric-patterned vellums! Use them underneath other geometric patterns, accents and more. Here, Annie added a bit of depth and richness with embroidered ribbon, **leading the eye** through the title. One of the coolest things on this page? Annie found a text pattern with a line about fairies. To emphasize those words, she traced directly over the top with a black pen, bringing the words forward within the design.

SUPPLIES *Textured cardstock:* Bazzill Basics Paper; *Patterned papers:* K&Company and 7gypsies; *Vellum:* My Mind's Eye; *Stickers:* EK Success, Making Memories; *Rub-ons:* Fontwerks and K&Company; *Journaling tags:* 7gypsies; *Tabs:* Scrapworks; *Pen:* EK Success; *Other:* Ribbon.

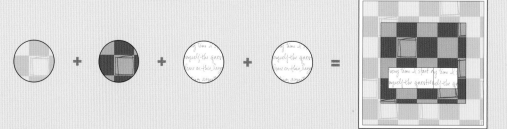

fall

2005

monday **pick up**
homework ✓
election Tuesday **school council**
tuesday **drop off**
religious education ✓✓
pick up
cancelled ~~**field trip**~~
swim league
wednesday
homework
drop off
remember books **singing**
↳**library day**
thursday
pick up
ho* work *finish*
off
ue
p
ics
p off
a* tia dance ✓
pickup
Saturday
german school

Some days I wonder
how my kids will turn out,
but most of the time
I'm just figuring out
how to survive them
RIGHT NOW
- storypeople

RIGHT NOW BY ANNIE WEIS

why this works: *Go for the shape.* I love using patterns as a small part of my layouts. Here, Annie repeated the diamond pattern by cutting the paper into large diamond shapes. She added stitching on top of those shapes, anchoring them to the layout. In the upper-left corner, she added a large rub-on diamond pattern, **repeating the elements** in the bottom corner. Also, notice how she used her handwriting in conjunction with printed journaling—I love the look of the crossed-off list (embrace that imperfection) with additional little notes here and there. So representative of real life. Very, very cool.

SUPPLIES *Patterned papers:* Chatterbox, Scenic Route Paper Co. and Scrapworks; *Border stickers and ribbon:* Scrapworks; *Rub-ons:* Scenic Route Paper Co. and Fontwerks; *Mini tags, jump rings, ribbon and photo corners:* Heidi Swapp for Advantus; *Computer fonts:* Georgia, downloaded from the Internet; *Pen:* American Crafts; *Other:* Quote from www.storypeople.com.

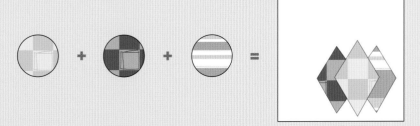

designer insight

You've got an awesome stash of patterned papers you've picked up at your local store because you loved them and you just had to have them. And that's perfectly, wonderfully okay. Now, here's a little tip: if you organize those papers, you'll know what you have in your stash. And trust me, knowing what you have is the first step to being able to use what you have. Here are three quick tips for storing and organizing your patterned paper:

1. *I use a 12" x 12" tower from Display Dynamics to store my patterned paper by manufacturer.* I like seeing the papers out in the open—it helps me remember what's available to me when I scrapbook. I also know many scrapbookers who organize their patterned papers by color or pattern (circle, stripe, text and so on). Organize your papers in any way that is meaningful and helpful to you.

2. *I love scraps.* I love to have them all mixed up together in one location. It's one of the areas of my scrap life where I'm not completely organized—and I'm okay with that (if you've taken one of my classes, you know one of my key phrases is, *"It is okay"*). My scrap pieces of patterned paper are stashed in one big box under my scrap table, so they're easily accessible when I'm putting layouts together (another key in using scraps is having them close at hand).

3. *Sort regularly.* When I started working on this book, I went through all my patterned papers and was so surprised and delighted by the patterns I rediscovered. I'd forgotten about papers that were hiding in my stash! Finding "new" stuff made me feel inspired and energized, and ready to get down to business.

100% CUTE BY ALI EDWARDS

why this works: Here, I created blocks of patterns that are the same size as my photos and distributed them evenly across and down my layout for a crisp, clean design. Rub-on stitching brings the whole thing together. Plus, the three flower accents on top of the patterns create a **visual triangle**.

SUPPLIES *Textured cardstock:* Bazzill Basics Paper; *Patterned papers:* Mara-Mi (stripes); Scrapworks (geometric); Danny O (geometric), K&Company; *Rubber stamp:* Fontwerks; *Stamping ink:* Ranger Industries; *Printed postcard:* 7gypsies; *Rub-on stitching:* Fontwerks; *Tab:* Narratives, Creative Imaginations; *Rub-on quote:* Die Cuts With a View; *Pen:* American Crafts; *Other:* Flowers.

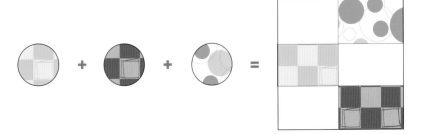

JOY OF YOU BY ALI EDWARDS

why this works: Geometric patterned paper works well with geometric photo blocks. On this layout, I added a couple of small circle accents for **contrast**. *Tip:* Cut rub-ons apart—see the dateline on the right-hand side of the layout—and use the interior section for journaling or additional accents.

SUPPLIES *Textured cardstock:* Bazzill Basics Paper; *Patterned papers:* Chatterbox (geometric) and Scenic Route Paper Co. (text); *Circle sticker:* Die Cuts With a View; *Rub-ons:* Dee's Designs, My Mind's Eye; *Word stickers:* K&Company; *Long, raised sticker:* Christina Cole for Provo Craft; *Pen:* Creative Memories; *Corner rounder:* Marvy Uchida; *Other:* Clocks.

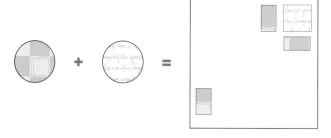

chapter summary

CHAPTER 5: GEOMETRIC

1. *Establish direction on your page by using diamond shapes to move the eye.*

2. *Convey a sense of energy, motion and fun with large geometric prints.*

3. *Create a formal look and feel on your page with black-and-white geometric patterns.*

4. *Cut geometric paper into shapes and use them as accents on your layout.*

5. *Pair geometric paper with geometric photo blocks for a balanced page.*

6. *Position page accents inside square and rectangle blocks.*

7. *Choose a geometric shape (such as a square) and repeat it in various sizes on your page.*

CKU

2005

STAMFORD, CT

THE REAL ALI ? please stand up...

October 2005. Where the heck am I? A bunch of very cool women from the East Coast decided it would be fun to create a dorm at CKU-A Stamford

of "Ali Impersonators." *It was hilarious*. Green cardigans. Thick glasses. Blondish wigs. And lots and lots of A's. Gotta love that spirit. One of the things

I love about CKU is that it gives women a chance to let go of the pressures of home and just play and and create and be silly. *Nice job ladies*.

life is here and now... either we meet it, we live it or we miss it. All life resides in the narrow margin and broad expanse of the moment. It is the doing, the dreaming, the feeling and the caring. It is always present in a glorious attempt, a lofty dream, a brilliant insight, an irreplaceable experience, a calming breath, an unbelievable feeling and an irrepressible passion.

Kobi Yamada

challenges
PATTERNED PAPER

One of the most effective ways I've found to try something new is to engage myself in a challenge. I'm not big on lots of pressure, but I do like the opportunity to explore and play, and challenges tend to steer me in that direction.

This chapter is going to be all about stretching yourself. Getting out of your ordinary scrapbooking routine. Some of the challenges may really make you think; others may be as simple as looking at a familiar technique in a new way.

You can do this.

Have fun with it. Get together with some buddies and work on the challenges together. Challenge friends online to play.

And before you dismiss anything, give it a try. I would love to see your results!

THE REAL ALI BY ALI EDWARDS

SUPPLIES ON OPPOSITE PAGE *Textured cardstock:* Bazzill Basics Paper; *Patterned paper:* Jeneva & Company; *Rub-on letters:* BasicGrey and Making Memories; *Rub-on stitching:* Autumn Leaves; *Rubber stamp:* Fontwerks; *Acrylic paint:* Making Memories; *Computer font:* Baskerville, downloaded from the Internet.

9 SQUARES *challenge*

TREASURE BY JAMIE WATERS

the challenge: Go to your scraps. Close your eyes (this takes the problem of choice and too much thinking out of the equation). Pull out six pieces of patterned paper that are big enough to be square-punched. Punch one square from each scrap. Now punch three photos. Place all nine squares together on a 12" x 12" piece of cardstock. Journal around the outside of your square. Voilà—a wonderful example of a completely random pattern assortment!

SUPPLIES *Patterned papers:* Daisy D's Paper Co., KI Memories, Autumn Leaves and BasicGrey; *Ribbon:* May Arts and Li'l Davis Designs; *Rhinstone buckle, epoxy letter and metal holder:* Li'l Davis Designs; *Plastic tab:* Creative Imaginations; *Rub-on:* Making Memories.

JUST BECAUSE BY VANESSA REYES

SUPPLIES *Patterned papers:* Making Memories, EK Success, Scrap in a Snap and Provo Craft; *Letter stickers:* American Crafts; *Photo corners:* Chatterbox; *Clip:* Artistic Expressions; *Crystal brad:* Making Memories; *Large photo corners:* Heidi Swapp for Advantus; *Flower sticker:* Christina Cole for Provo Craft.

ANGLED PAPER *challenge*

BACKYARD BOY BY ALI EDWARDS

the challenge: Instead of cutting everything into squares and rectangles, take an angular approach! Take a large photograph and cut the bottom at an angle. Use ribbons to define the edges of the photograph. Stack layers of triangular paper underneath the photo to create a playful look on your page.

SUPPLIES *Patterned papers:* 7gypsies, Anna Griffin, Mustard Moon, Making Memories and Li'l Davis Designs; *Acetate:* 7gypsies; *Pen:* Zig Millennium, EK Success; *Letter stickers:* Source unknown; *Other:* Ribbon, staples and rub-ons.

CREATE YOUR OWN ART PRINT *challenge*

ART @ AGE 3 BY ALI EDWARDS

the challenge: Art patterns can also be "real life" art. One of my favorite ways to display Simon's art is to turn it into patterned paper. Here, I combined his handprints (which is art in itself!) with the art his hands created. Go ahead—experiment. Create your own art prints!

SUPPLIES *Textured cardstock:* Bazzill Basics Paper; *Tag and stickers:* 7gypsies; *Rubber stamps:* Turtle Press and PSX Design; *Stamping ink:* ColorBox Fluid Chalk, Clearsnap; *Pen:* American Crafts.

MODIFIED CIRCLE *challenge*

MORNING COFFEE BY ALI EDWARDS

the challenge: Use just a bit of pattern as an add-on to a circle. Choose two patterns with coordinating colors (these both have a gray-beige tone), punch and tear them, and adhere them to a punched circle. It's a great way to get a bit of pattern onto a layout.

SUPPLIES *Textured cardstock:* Bazzill Basics Paper; *Patterned papers:* Magic Scraps (circles) and Cross-My-Heart (art); *Circle punch:* McGill; *Letter and word stickers:* Chatterbox; *Rub-on:* foof-a-La, Autumn Leaves; *Fabric tape:* 7gypsies; *Pens:* Creative Memories; Zig Millennium, EK Success.

OFF CENTER *challenge*

SO MANY ME'S BY ALI EDWARDS

the challenge: Notice the off-center placement of the large rectangle (it includes everything within the boundaries of the photo corners). Off-center placement tends to be more "active" within a design. I grounded the rectangle by layering the title circle on top.

SUPPLIES *Textured cardstock:* Bazzill Basics Paper; *Patterned papers:* Cross-My-Heart (art) and Magic Scraps (circles); *Ribbon:* May Arts; *Word tags:* K&Company; *Silver flower accents:* Heidi Swapp for Advantus; *Circle punch:* McGill; *Stamping ink:* Stampin' Up!; *Date stamp:* Staples; *Blue pen:* American Crafts.

QUILTED-LOOK SCRAPS *challenge*

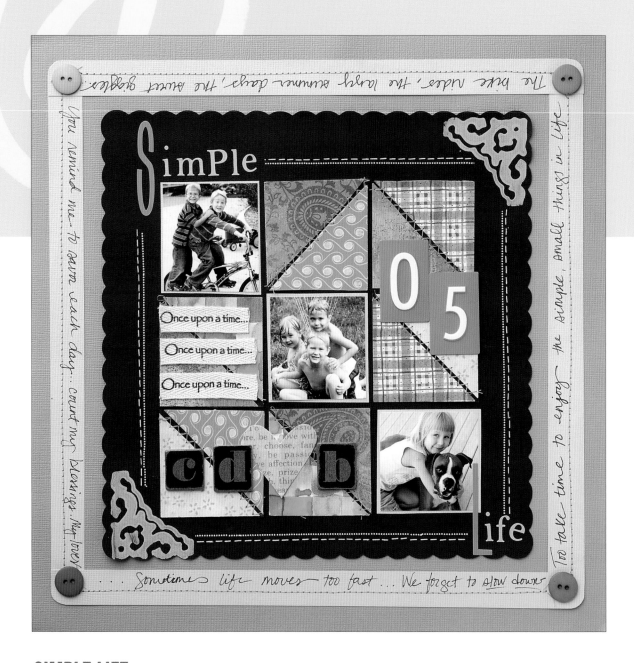

SIMPLE LIFE BY MILEY JOHNSON

the challenge: Cut triangular scraps of patterned paper and stitch them together to create a quilted look on your page. It's another great way to use those patterned-paper scraps!

SUPPLIES *Patterned papers:* Creative Imaginations, Provo Craft, Anna Griffin, Berry Patch, BasicGrey and Pebbles Inc.; *Letter stickers:* Chatterbox; *Metal numbers and foam stamps:* Making Memories; *Wooden letters:* Li'l Davis Designs; *Acrylic paint:* Delta Technical Coatings; *Buttons:* Junkitz; *Square punch:* Family Treasures; *Transparency:* 3M; *Pen:* EK Success.

SEVEN DIFFERENT PRINTS *challenge*

AUGUST 2005 BY ALI EDWARDS

the challenge: I combined seven different prints to create this page background! Notice how each print connects to the one above it or below it—they all work together as a cohesive group to unify the page.

SUPPLIES *Patterned papers:* My Mind's Eye, 7gypsies, KI Memories and Sweetwater; *Rub-on:* KI Memories; *Tab:* 7gypsies; *Stamping ink:* ColorBox, Clearsnap; *Computer fonts:* Vell MT and Bell Gothic, downloaded from the Internet; *Other:* Staple.

STENCIL SHAPE *challenge*

ZAFT BY ANNIE WEIS

the challenge: Have stencils (or die-cut shapes) in your scrapbook stash? Use them as a guide for cutting embellishments from your scraps of patterned paper, like these cool flowers.

SUPPLIES *Textured cardstock:* Bazzill Basics Paper; *Patterned papers:* Scenic Route Paper Co. and Scrapworks; *Stickers:* American Crafts and Mustard Moon; *Rubber stamps:* Fontwerks; *Stamping ink:* ColorBox, Clearsnap; *Rub-ons:* Scrapworks; *Concho:* 7gypsies; *Other:* Masking tape.

CLEAR BUTTON *challenge*

WONDER BY VANESSA REYES

the challenge: Transform plain, clear buttons into page accents with your circle punch. Just layer clear buttons over circle-punched patterned papers. It's a great way to use extra stuff from your stash or to create a super-coordinated look for your page.

SUPPLIES *Patterned papers:* Chatterbox and K&Company; *Clear buttons:* Autumn Leaves; *Rub-ons:* Scrapworks; *Letter stamps:* Educational Insights; *Photo corners:* Chatterbox.

MINI BOOK *challenge*

THE WIGGLES MINI BOOK BY ALI EDWARDS

the challenge: Print journaling on patterned paper to be used in a mini book. You'll find lots of patterned papers that are great for journaling (either handwritten or printed). Find one you love! Use additional scraps from your scrap stash for the punched-circle accents.

SUPPLIES *Album:* SEI; *Two-fold fastener:* Magic Scraps; *Patterned papers:* MOD (orange), Autumn Leaves; Scenic Route Paper Co. (green); KI Memories (stripes); Making Memories (stripes); *Sandpaper:* Heidi Swapp for Advantus; *Rub-ons:* Li'l Davis Designs; *Word stickers:* Wordsworth; *Computer font:* Times, downloaded from the Internet; *Rubber stamp:* 7gypsies; *Stamping ink:* Stampin' Up!; *Circle punch:* Marvy Uchida.

PAINTED BRIDGE *challenge*

20 PUMPKINS BY ALI EDWARDS

the challenge: Need an easy way to unify four different patterns? I used acrylic paint to stencil the number 20 across the patterns on the bottom of my page. The "20" acts as a bridge that pulls all four patterns together. Try it—you'll see!

SUPPLIES *Patterned papers:* 7gypsies, Anna Griffin, Mustard Moon, Making Memories and Li'l Davis Designs; *Acetate:* 7gypsies; *Pen:* Zig Millennium, EK Success; *Other:* Ribbon, staples, letter stickers and rub-ons.

BOY BY VANESSA REYES

the challenge: Weave several pieces of patterned paper together to create a page accent or a mat for a photograph or journaling.

SUPPLIES *Textured cardstock:* Bazzill Basics Paper; *Patterned papers:* Petals & Possibilities, KI Memories and Urban Lily; *Letter stickers, flower sticker, green rub-ons and metal letters:* KI Memories; *Metal-rimmed tag, foam stamp, safety pin, staples and rub-ons:* Making Memories; *Rub-on quotes:* Die Cuts With a View; *Twill and sticker strip:* 7gypsies; *Round bookplate:* Li'l Davis Designs; *Acetate flower:* Heidi Swapp for Advantus; *Metal plate:* American Crafts; *Paper flowers:* Prima; *Tab:* SEI; *Letter stamps:* PSX Design and Educational Insights; *Stamping ink:* ColorBox, Clearsnap; *Ribbon:* May Arts, Making Memories and Li'l Davis Designs.

RECTANGULAR BORDER *challenge*

ARE WE THERE YET? BY ALI EDWARDS

the challenge: Create a page border with scraps of patterned paper. Just cut eight patterned-paper scraps into rectangles and line them up in a row. Those rectangular pieces of paper make great homes for your journaling and page titles, too.

SUPPLIES *Patterned papers:* Imagination Project, EK Success, My Mind's Eye, K&Company and Sweetwater; *Wooden tags:* Chatterbox; *Acrylic paint:* Making Memories; *Other:* Rub-on letters.

MEMORIES OF GUAM BY VANESSA REYES

the challenge: Okay, this page looks really complex. But the secret is that it really isn't. Think of the page as one big, blank canvas. And then, imagine the canvas divided into two-thirds (the photographs) and one-third (the title, journaling and accents). Now, look at how Vanessa filled the one-third column with a variety of items that help tell her story. Try this when you have lots of memorabilia to fit onto one layout.

SUPPLIES *Patterned paper and vellum rub-ons:* Chatterbox; *Chipboard letters and photo corners:* Heidi Swapp for Advantus; *Twill, sticker and tag:* 7gypsies; *Crystal brad:* Making Memories; *Rub-ons:* 7gypsies and Making Memories; *Round tag:* Scrapworks; *Paper flower:* Prima; *Other:* Fabric and metal sheet.

MINI BOOK *challenge 2*

BOO 2004 BY ALI EDWARDS

the challenge: Enlarge a photo so it becomes a pattern. When you take pictures, don't forget to see the patterns in our world. Fields, fruits, faces, books and more can all be seen as patterns depending on how you take the photo. Here, a close-up shot of a pumpkin becomes a cool pattern when enlarged and cropped close. Use your enlarged pattern photo as the opener for a mini book. Utilize those great little contact sheets from your photo developer by cutting them up and layering them right on top of your patterned photo.

SUPPLIES *File folder:* Autumn Leaves; *Patterned papers:* Scrapworks (circles) and 7gypsies (floral); *Textured cardstock:* Bazzill Basics Paper; *Fabric tags:* Scrapworks; *Ribbon:* American Crafts; *Corner rounder:* Marvy Uchida; *Stamping ink:* Stampin' Up!; *Clear envelopes:* Deluxe Designs.

PATTERNED-PAPER
EMBELLISHMENT *challenge*

MY GIRL BY VANESSA REYES

the challenge: Vanessa is the master of cutting embellishments from patterned paper and using them to accent her pages. On these pages, you'll see where she's cut small flowers and layered them over large flowers. You'll see where she's cut flowers from patterned paper and then layered clear buttons and metal embellishments over the flowers. And, notice how she's even layered flowers over flowers (she used pop dots to add dimension). Your challenge is to follow Vanessa's lead and look for accents you can cut from paper and use on your pages.

SUPPLIES *Patterned papers:* Autumn Leaves and Petals & Possibilities; *Die cuts and buttons:* Autumn Leaves; *Bookplate:* Li'l Davis Designs; *Letter stickers:* Chatterbox, American Crafts and Heidi Grace Designs; *Rub-ons:* Scrapworks; *Metal plates:* American Crafts; *Sticker strip:* 7gypsies; *Ribbon:* May Arts; *Cardstock tag:* Making Memories; *Photo corners:* Chatterbox.

EXPLORER OF SO MUCH

BY VANESSA REYES

SUPPLIES *Patterned papers:* Autumn Leaves, Mustard Moon, Imagination Project and Daisy D's Paper Co.; *Transparency:* K&Company; *Die cut, twill, tab, rub-ons and clear letter:* Autumn Leaves; *Word strip:* Christina Cole for Provo Craft; *Crystal brads and rub-ons:* Making Memories; *Ribbon:* May Arts; *Paper flower:* Prima; *Photo corners:* Maya Road; *Other:* Magnifying glass and handmade paper.

TWIRL BY VANESSA REYES

SUPPLIES *Patterned papers, chipboard letters and flower cutouts:* Chatterbox; *Clear letter and clear stickers:* Autumn Leaves; *Die cut and clear buttons:* Autumn Leaves; *Canvas frame:* Li'l Davis Designs; *Conchos:* Scrapworks; *Market tag:* Pebbles Inc.; *Acrylic paint:* Delta Technical Coatings; *Rub-ons:* KI Memories; *Ribbon:* May Arts and Li'l Davis Designs; *Other:* Heart brad and textured paper.

UNBREAKABLE BY VANESSA REYES

SUPPLIES *Patterned papers and stickers:* Chatterbox; *Tape, metal tab and tag:* 7gypsies; *Circle sticker:* Christina Cole for Provo Craft; *Transparency:* K&Company; *Ribbon:* May Arts and Making Memories; *Letter stamps:* PSX Design; *Stamping ink:* ColorBox, Clearsnap; *Other:* Vintage trim.

MINI BOOK *challenge 3*

LOVE LOVE LOVE BY ALI EDWARDS

the challenge: *Light and dark.* Bring two light patterns and two dark patterns together in the same project. Free-hand cut or punch each pattern into small squares. Repeat these patterns on the four large tags (covering both the front and back), then add 2" x 2" photos to the large tags. Journal on the back of each page in the mini book.

SUPPLIES *Mini book:* Making Memories; *Textured cardstock:* Bazzill Basics Paper; *Patterned papers:* 7gypsies (text and floral) and Chatterbox (floral and stripe); *Ribbon:* May Arts; *Round tags:* EK Success; *Pens:* American Crafts; *Index tabs:* OfficeMax.

IMPERFECTLY MATCHED
COLORS *challenge*

LOVE IS THE GOLDEN THREAD

THAT TIES OUR **HEARTS** AND **SOULS** TOGETHER.
{MOTHER TERESA}

THE GOLDEN THREAD BY ALI EDWARDS

the challenge: Tie a variety of patterned tags together by using different shades of the same color. Let go of that need to have the colors match perfectly. Tear each of the tags, vary their length, and place them behind a gathering of photos. Stamp small white tags with date stamps and attach them to the patterned tags with brads.

SUPPLIES *Textured cardstock:* Bazzill Basics Paper; *Patterned tags:* SEI, BasicGrey and Scrapworks; *Rubber stamps:* Stampin' Up!; *Stamping ink:* VersaColor, Tsukineko; *Rub-on heart circle:* KI Memories; *Rub-on quote:* Die Cuts With a View; *Brads:* Making Memories; *Pen:* American Crafts.

GOODNESS
LEARN FROM
YOUR MISTAKES
SEEK **TRUTH** AND
SPREAD **JOY**

EMBRACE YOUR

GOODNESS

LEARN FROM

YOUR MISTAKES

SEEK **TRUTH** AND

SPREAD **JOY**

EMBRACE YOUR
GOODNESS
LEARN FROM
YOUR MISTAKES
SEEK **TRUTH** AND
SPREAD **JOY**

EMBRACE YOUR
GOODNESS
LEARN FROM
YOUR MISTAKES
SEEK **TRUTH** AND
SPREAD **JOY**

EMBRACE YOUR

GOODNESS

LEARN FROM

YOUR MISTAKES

SEEK **TRUTH** AND

SPREAD **JOY**

EMBRACE YOUR

GOODNESS

LEARN FROM

YOUR MISTAKES

SEEK **TRUTH** AND